WORLDS OF WONDER

Resources for Multicultural
Children's Literature

Paula Kezwer

Pippin Publishing

Copyright © 1995 Pippin Publishing Corporation
85 Ellesmere Road
Suite 232
Scarborough, Ontario
M1R 4B9

All rights reserved. No part of this publication may be reproduced or transmitted in any form or by any means, electronic, mechanical, or otherwise, including photocopying and recording, or stored in any retrieval system without permission in writing from the publisher.

The publishers and artists who granted permission to photograph the covers of books are gratefully acknowledged.

Edited by Dyanne Rivers
Designed by John Zehethofer
Printed and bound in Canada by Friesens Corporation

Canadian Cataloguing in Publication Data
Kezwer, Paula
    Worlds of wonder

Includes bibliographical references.
ISBN 0-88751-065-5

1. Children's literature - Bibliography. 2. Minorities - Juvenile literature - Bibliography. 3. Manners and customs - Juvenile literature - Bibliography. 4. Tales - Bibliography. 5. Children - Books and reading. I. Title.

Z1037.K48   100.62   C95-930750-8

ISBN 0-88751-065-5

10   9   8   7   6   5   4   3   2

For my children, Matan and Bareket,
who have taught me so much
about both the substance and spirit of diversity.

Among the many colleagues and friends who assisted and encouraged me in this project, I would particularly like to thank the following: Theo Hersh and the helpful staff of the Forest Hill Branch of the Toronto Public Library for their cheerful help with my hundreds of reserve requests and inquiries; Michael de Gale of Perception II Multicultural Books for introducing me to many wonderful new works; Jonathan Lovat Dickson of Pippin Publishing for believing in my idea; Dyanne Rivers for her thorough editing work; the many book publishers across North America who supplied review copies and permissions; my colleagues and friends at the Etobicoke Board of Education who are a constant source of inspiration and ideas for working with kids, teachers and books; and, finally, my parents, Sara Markus and the late Bernard Markus, who instilled a love of learning and reading that has always stayed with me.

Contents

Introduction 7

The Immigrant Experience
The African Heritage 13
The Chinese Experience 26
The European Experience 30
The Hispanic Experience 33
The Japanese Experience 41
The Korean Experience 45
The South Asian Experience 48
The Southeast Asian Experience 50

The World Over
Africa 57
Canada 64
Caribbean 70
Central and South America 81
China 87
Eastern Europe 92
The First Peoples of North America 104
Japan 112
The Jewish Experience 121
Korea 130
The Middle East 135
South Asia 144
Southeast Asia 151
Various Cultures in a Single Book 158
Western Europe 169

Indexes
Index—Authors 179
Index—Titles 199
Index—Themes 209

Introduction

During the 1990s, teachers have become increasingly responsive to the cultural diversity reflected in their classrooms. Educators now realize the benefits of acknowledging in the curriculum the varied groups that make up our society. When a cross-section of multicultural perspectives permeates the curriculum, it validates all students' lives. It helps learners recognize the universal values that are common to all cultures, as well as appreciate the rich and positive differences between cultures.

Contemporary educators acknowledge how important it is for young people to "see themselves" in the curriculum and in the books it encompasses. Paradoxically, multicultural books facilitate the integration of immigrant children into the mainstream culture of their adopted homeland.

More and more teachers are recognizing that the infusion of diverse voices is among the most important contributions they can make to young peoples' education. But teachers are often at a loss about where to find appropriate resources to present a multicultural classroom perspective.

In my work as co-ordinator of the English as a second language program for a large Ontario school board, I am constantly approached by teachers of all grade levels seeking suggestions for inclusionary classroom resources. There is a dearth of easily accessible reference books that inform teachers about and direct them to multicultural children's literature. In response to this need, I began compiling this book.

Over the last several years, I've had the pleasure of reading and reviewing hundreds of multicultural children's books, everything from picture books to folktales, from chapter books for middle graders to coming-of-age novels with mature themes. The more than 320 annotated entries in this book represent my personal choices of exemplary multicultural children's literature, strong in both literary and artistic merit, as well as cultural accuracy.

With the plethora of outstanding books currently on the market, many readers may come across excellent books that are not included here. The absence of a citation is not intended as a judgment of any one book. This volume is not designed to be a definitive listing. The omissions are all my own.

In organizing this book, I divided it into three parts. The first is titled "The Immigrant Experience" and is broken down into chapters dealing with the experiences of members of various cultural groups as they mingle with the North American mainstream. The second, titled "The World Over," is divided into chapters according to the global geographic region and culture of origin of the stories. It's worth noting that deciding where to list books wasn't always straightforward. When this was the case, I arbitrarily selected a chapter that seemed appropriate, though equally compelling arguments might be made for placing some books elsewhere. The third part is the indexes, which list the books according to title, author and theme.

Each citation in the first two parts supplies basic bibliographical data about the book to facilitate the borrowing or purchase of the resource. As well, each book is categorized according to its age appropriateness. Teachers should note, however, that the suggested age ranges are meant as a guide only. Creative educators will find many uses for these books with learners of English as a second language of any age, including adults.

Multicultural literature should form an integral part of reading and studies across the curriculum. The third index categorizes many of the books reviewed into 18 cross-curricular theme areas representing some of the most commonly conceived subject themes in both elementary and secondary schools. In this way, teachers can ensure that diverse cultural voices are easily integrated into their theme studies.

Of course, aside from specific curricular connections, all educators will want to ensure that their school resource centers, classroom libraries, listening centers, book corners and read-aloud programs also contain a wide variety of multicultural choices. Family literacy and book-borrowing programs are other areas that can benefit from an infusion of multicultural resources.

Educators interested in pursuing in greater depth strategies for teaching multicultural literature and developing cross-cultural awareness will find the following works helpful:

Allen, Judy, Eldene McNeill & Velma Schmidt. *Cultural Awareness for Children*. Reading, Mass.: Addison-Wesley, 1992.

Harris, Violet J. *Teaching Multicultural Literature in Grades K-8*. Norwood, Mass.: Christopher-Gordon Publishers, 1993.
Jobe, Ron. *Cultural Connections: Using Literature to Explore World Cultures with Children*. Markham, Ontario: Pembroke Press, 1993.
York, Stacey. *Roots and Wings: Affirming Culture in Early Childhood Programs*. St. Paul, Minn.: Redleaf Press, 1991.

Finally, this book will also make an invaluable contribution to teachers of adult ESL learners as they discover the joy of using children's literature with their grown-up students. Because many children's picture books address mature themes or carry universal appeal, a wise selection of picture books will ensure that no adult learner feels condescended to in the classroom. Encouraging these students to participate in comparative folk and fairy tale studies, write their own picture books and stories, and develop their vocabulary by creating sophisticated alphabet and picture books along the lines of Ruth Wells' *From A to Zen* (see page 120) are just some of the many multicultural literature activities that appeal to older ESL learners.

It is my hope that this book will help enrich your classroom program and the students' lives and, in its own small way, contribute to understanding and peace among all of us.

Paula Kezwer
Toronto, 1995

The Immigrant Experience

The African Heritage

Battle-Lavert, Gwendolyn
The Barber's Cutting Edge
Illustrated by Raymond Holbert
Children's Book Press, 1994
Ages 5-8, unpaged
ISBN 0-89239-127-8

Rashaad likes to have his hair cut by the best barber in town, Mr. Bigelow, who can masterfully create any style, from college cut to gumby. When Rashaad brings his vocabulary definitions to study while perched on the barber's chair, he challenges Mr. Bigelow to come up with the meanings of some mighty difficult words. Stumped by a particularly perplexing bit of English, Mr. Bigelow sneaks into the back room to pore over the dictionary—his cutting edge as far as language is concerned. The snappy text and bright illustrations of this jauntily written book capture a young boy's mentor passing on his respect for learning to the next generation.

Bunting, Eve
Smoky Night
Illustrated by David Diaz
Harcourt Brace Jovanovich, 1994
Ages 8 and up, unpaged
ISBN 0-15-269954-6

The riots that occurred in Los Angeles in 1992 after the Rodney King trial provide the setting for this book, which deals sensitively with a number of difficult issues. With his mother, Daniel, a young black boy, is peering out his apartment window at the rioting masses below. When their building is engulfed by flames and they must abandon their apartment for an emergency shelter, both learn a valuable lesson about getting along with others, no matter what their background. This book deals squarely with the complex issue of interracial prejudice among ethnic minorities, a subject not often broached in children's literature. The artwork is also exceptional. The montage photographs of spilled groceries, cut glass and goods in disarray placed below the text suggest the chaos and senseless destruction of the rioting. *Smoky Night* is a provocative book that can be used in a variety of ways as a springboard to discussion and as a useful tool in anti-bias education from the junior grades up.

Feelings, Tom
Soul Looks Back in Wonder
Dial Books, 1993
Ages 8 and up, unpaged
ISBN 0-8037-1001-1

After completing the bold and moving artwork for this book, illustrator Tom Feelings invited black American poets to compose original works for the anthology. The result is a stunning collection of 13 poems, each written in a unique style that celebrates the African heritage. Selections such as the rap-style "Boyz n Search of Their Soular System" by Eugene B. Redmond and the lyrical "I Love the Look of Words" by Maya Angelou give this anthology a feel of unity in reveling in black America's legacy, past and future. Winner of the 1994 Coretta Scott King Award for best illustrator.

In a bumper year for the genre, *Brown Honey in Broomwheat Tea* (HarperCollins, 1993: ISBN 0-06-021087-7), another outstanding poetry book celebrating the black experience, was a Coretta Scott King Honor Book for both author Joyce Carol Thomas and illustrator Floyd Cooper.

Hamilton, Virginia
Many Thousand Gone
Illustrated by Leo and Diane Dillon
Knopf, 1993
Ages 8-14, 152 pp.
ISBN 0-394-82873-9 (hardcover)
      0-394-92873-3 (paperback)

This groundbreaking work traces the history of American slaves' attempts to gain freedom, from the earliest days of the slave trade through the rise of the Underground Railroad to the declaration of the Emancipation Proclamation. Carefully researched and written, *Many Thousand Gone* relates this history as it should be told, through the first-person narratives of those who actually lived through the experience. Individual profiles of well-known figures such as Harriet Tubman, Sojourner Truth and Frederick Douglass are presented. But there are also those whose voices have been less frequently heard—Henry Box Brown, who built a wooden crate and delivered himself to freedom via the U.S. Mail, and Jackson, who came north disguised as a lady's maid. The Dillons' black-and-white block print illustrations add to the dignity and power of this extraordinary historical account, which was an American Library Association Notable Children's Book in 1994.

By the same author-illustrator team is the excellent *The People Could Fly* (Knopf, 1985: ISBN 0-679-84336-1, paperback), a collection of African-American folktales of the animal world, the supernatural, and the desire for freedom.

Hamilton, Virginia
Drylongso
Harcourt Brace Jovanovich, 1992
Ages 8-12, 56 pp.
ISBN 0-15-224241-4

Thought to be rooted in the African Gullah language as it became creolized during the period of slavery in the southern United States, *drylongso* means drought. Later, it also came to describe something ordinary and dull that dragged on always the same, seemingly forever. This story takes place in the farmlands west of the Mississippi River during a drought in the mid-1970s. A terrible dust storm envelops the farms and buildings, and when the grit begins to settle, a young boy named Drylongso seems to have blown in with it. Drylongso can divine for water and, with his dowser, he is able to help one struggling family gain a foothold against the scorching drought. Drylongso disappears without saying goodbye, but the mythic, folkloric figure leaves his divining stick behind as a symbol of hope for better times.

Hill, Lawrence
Trials and Triumphs: The Story of African-Canadians
Umbrella Press, 1993
Ages 10-16, 64 pp.
ISBN 1-895642-09-4 (paperback)
      1-895642-10-9 (hardcover)

Like *Leading the Way* (see page 23), this book offers a much-needed introduction for young people to the history and contributions of black Canadians. *Trials and Triumphs* offers an overview of African Canadian history from the earliest beginnings of slavery in New France and English Canada, to the gradual end of slavery in the early 19th century, to the Underground Railroad whose terminus was in Canada in the decade before the American Civil War. The history of black immigration to Canada, the establishment of the Caribbean Canadian community and the contributions of many celebrated African Canadian personalities are all covered in this well-designed and accessible book.

Hoffman, Mary
Amazing Grace
Illustrated by Caroline Binch
Dial Books for Young Readers, 1991
Ages 4-8, unpaged
ISBN 0-8037-1040-2 (hardcover)
     0-71-120699-6 (paperback—Frances Lincoln)

Grace has a flair for the dramatic and loves to dress up and pretend she is Joan of Arc, Mowgli the Jungle Boy, or the captain of a pirate ship sailing the high seas. When her friends aren't around, it doesn't matter— Grace just acts all the parts herself. One day, Grace's teacher announces that the class will stage *Peter Pan*, but Grace is intimidated when one of her classmates whispers, "You can't be Peter Pan. He wasn't black." With the support of her mother and grandmother, Grace learns that she can do anything she sets her mind to. The movement and color of Caroline Binch's illustrations burst off the page, effectively conveying Grace's head-on approach to life.

Hopkinson, Deborah
Sweet Clara and the Freedom Quilt
Illustrated by James Ransome
Knopf, 1993
Ages 6-10, unpaged
ISBN 0-679-82311-5

As a seamstress in the big house of the plantation, Clara appreciates that she is better off than the field slaves. But she dreams that she will be reunited with her mother from whom she has been separated and even that, together, they will run away north to freedom. One day, Clara overhears two slaves wishing they had a map so they could locate the Underground Railroad that would lead them north to freedom. In a flash of inspiration, she sees how to use the cloth collected in her scrap bag to stitch a map—a freedom quilt—that will be above the suspicion of any master. Unable to read or write, Clara uses all her resourcefulness, skills and courage to try to become the master of her own destiny. This book is a well-told, first-person account of the Underground Railroad that also makes a suspenseful read-aloud for younger readers.

Hudson, Wade (Ed.)
Pass It On: African-American Poetry for Children
Illustrated by Floyd Cooper
Scholastic, 1993
Ages 6-10, unpaged
ISBN 0-590-45770-5

Poetry is an important part of the African-American oral tradition, and each of the carefully selected short poems in this volume interprets an aspect of the black American experience. The collection includes works by outstanding black American poets, including Langston Hughes and Eloise Greenfield. The illustrations complement the poems without overpowering the text, which can be enjoyed by children and adults of all backgrounds.

Johnson, Angela
Toning the Sweep
Orchard Books, 1993
Ages 10-16, 103 pp.
ISBN 0-531-05476-4 (hardcover)
       0-590-48142-8 (paperback—Scholastic)

According to an old folk custom among blacks in the southern United States, when someone died, a relative would take a hammer and strike a sweep, a type of plow, to spread the news of the death. "Toning the sweep" was also a way of ushering the dead person's soul to heaven. In this moving story of discoveries made by three generations of African American women, 14-year-old Emmie must deal with the impending death of her beloved grandmother, just as Emmie's mother must make peace with mourning her own father's passing, many years before. Winner of the 1994 Coretta Scott King Award.

Johnson, Angela
The Leaving Morning
Illustrated by David Soman
Orchard Books, 1992
Ages 4-7, unpaged
ISBN 0-531-05992-8

Moving house can be painful for children, as they say goodbye to the people and places that mean so much to them. This beautiful picture book relates the story of what happens when two young black children move away from their neighborhood. The children think of an expressive way to leave something special of themselves behind. Somehow, this seems to ease their regret at leaving behind friends, family and familiar places and helps them look forward to the new and unknown.

Lauture, Denize
Father and Son
Illustrated by Jonathan Green
Philomel Books, 1992
All ages, unpaged
ISBN 0-399-21867-X

Father and Son is Haitian poet Denize Lauture's first book for children. In spare but beautiful verse, Lauture describes how a father and son share special time together as they walk down country roads, follow their shadows along the beach, read together on a lazy porch swing and sing out in church. The fabulous, richly toned illustrations are from a series of oil paintings by Jonathan Green, an American artist who draws heavily on his own heritage among the Gullah people of South Carolina. This lilting poem will be thoroughly enjoyed by children and adults alike.

Lawrence, Jacob
The Great Migration: An American Story
The Museum of Modern Art, The Phillips Collection, HarperCollins, 1993
Ages 8-12, unpaged
ISBN 0-06-023037-1

In 1940-1941, well-known African-American artist Jacob Lawrence painted a series of 60 individual panels chronicling the mass migration of black Americans from the rural South in search of employment in the industrial cities of the North during the First World

War. Split between New York's Museum of Modern Art and Washington, D.C.'s Phillips Collection, the cycle of paintings was reunited in 1993 for a traveling exhibition of Lawrence's work. The panels have been gathered in this book and combined with a spare, but powerful, text to present a commanding portrayal of the quintessential harshness and dignity of the migrant's search for a better life.

McKissack, Patricia C.
The Dark Thirty: Southern Tales of the Supernatural
Illustrated by Brian Pinkney
Knopf, 1992
Ages 9-12, 122 pp.
ISBN 0-679-81-863-4 (hardcover)
      0-590-47735-8 (paperback—Scholastic)

The Dark Thirty is a collection of spine-tingling tales rooted in the storytelling lore of African Americans. Through the medium of scary stories, McKissack imparts a wealth of information about the historical experiences of black Americans, from the origin of the first all-black union (railway porters) to the 1955 Montgomery, Alabama, bus boycott to the mysterious cures accomplished by roots and herbs that southern rural "conjure women" found in the earth. The eerie distinctiveness of the artwork was achieved by using a scratchboard technique, in which a white board covered with black ink is etched with a sharp tool to reveal the white underneath. Winner of the 1993 Coretta Scott King Award for best author.

McKissack, Patricia C.
Mirandy and Brother Wind
Illustrated by Jerry Pinkney
Knopf, 1988
Ages 6-10, unpaged
ISBN 0-394-88765

The cakewalk is a traditional African-American dance in which couples strut, kick and twirl around a large square dance floor as their performance is judged by the elders of the community. It takes its name from the cake that the winning pair took home as a prize. In this lively tale set in the turn-of-the-century rural American South, Mirandy sets out to win fleet-footed Brother Wind as her partner for her very first junior cakewalk. After chasing him through the woods and farms, she finally captures him and learns the true secret of his inspiration. Through its supernatural elements, good-humored dialogue in authentic dialect, and richly detailed watercolor illustrations, this engaging story captures the flavor of a moment in time in African-American culture and society.

Mirandy and Brother Wind is also available with an audiocassette of the story joyously narrated by actress Cicely Tyson to the accompaniment of cakewalk music. A Coretta Scott King Honor Book for illustration in 1989 as well as a Caldecott Honor Book.

Mitchell, Margaree King
Uncle Jed's Barbershop
Illustrated by James Ransome
Simon and Schuster, 1993
Ages 7-10, unpaged
ISBN 0-671-76969-3

During the days of segregation in the American South, Sarah Jean's Uncle Jed dreamed of opening his own barbershop. As the only black barber in the county, Uncle Jed toted his clippers to the homes of his customers, saving for the day when he would make his dream come true. But circumstances threw obstacles in his path, first in the form of costly emergency surgery for Sarah Jean, and then in a bank failure. Finally, at 79, he achieves his goal, and the grown-up Sarah Jean is there to share in the joy of perseverance rewarded. James Ransome's warm illustrations of family life in the rural South complement the text, which provides an excellent springboard to a discussion of segregation and civil rights movements in the United States and elsewhere. A 1994 Coretta Scott King honor book for illustration.

Myers, Walter Dean
Brown Angels
HarperCollins, 1993
All ages, unpaged
ISBN 0-06-022918-7

Antique photographs of African-American children from the author's own extensive collection form the stunning centerpiece of this volume of poetry celebrating childhood and love. The poems are brief and satisfying, but it is the extraordinary glimpses of childhood as expressed in the smiling, pouting, joyful, wondering and exuberant faces of the children that will lure readers to pore over and discuss this unique book.

Paulsen, Gary
Nightjohn
Delacorte Press, 1993
Ages 12 and up, 92 pp.
ISBN 0-385-30838-8 (hardcover)
     0-440-21936-1 (paperback—Bantam Doubleday Dell)

From Newbery Award-winning author Gary Paulsen comes this brief but powerful novel told in the voice and authentic dialect of Sarny, a young slave girl. Sarny secretly begins learning to read when she is tutored by the new field hand, John, whom the master has recently bought. After escaping via the Underground Railroad to freedom in the North, John—or Nightjohn—learned to read and write, and returned to the South to set up clandestine nighttime schools in the woods for slaves. But he was caught before he could turn this dream into reality. Knowing that the penalty for learning to read is dismemberment and having seen her master punish other slaves harshly, Sarny still wants to take the risk and learn to read with Nightjohn. Readers will be held spellbound by this gripping story of Sarny's attempt to achieve "the way to know." The book contains graphic descriptions of brutality. Though they are in no way gratuitous, *Nightjohn* is not recommended for readers younger than 12. A 1994 American Library Association Best Book for Young Adults.

Polacco, Patricia
Mrs. Katz and Tush
Bantam Books, 1992
Ages 5-9, unpaged
ISBN 0-553-08122-5

Larnel doesn't know his neighbor, Mrs. Katz, very well until he asks her to adopt a stray kitten. Mrs. Katz agrees, on one condition: that Larnel help her take care of the pet that she names Tush. When Larnel starts spending more and more time with Mrs. Katz, taking care of Tush and sharing stories over pieces of freshly baked *kugel*, he begins to learn about her life in Poland before she immigrated to America and the Jewish traditions she brought with her to her new country. Larnel grows to love Mrs. Katz and, in the process, discovers the suffering and triumph that are common themes of both black and Jewish history. This heartwarming story bridges the gap between religions and generations and emphasizes the rich emotional connections between people that can transcend age and culture.

Ringgold, Faith
Dinner at Aunt Connie's House
Hyperion Books for Children, 1993
Ages 5-9, unpaged
ISBN 1-56282-425-2

Faith Ringgold, an African-American artist and professor of art, is well-known both for her painted story quilts and her illustrated books for children. *Dinner at Aunt Connie's House* is based on "The Dinner Quilt," a story quilt Ringgold crafted in 1986. Adapted for children in this new book, the quilt commemorated the lives and accomplishments of 12 visionary black women and their contribution to American history. Ringgold sets out the depictions of the quilt in a magical storybook format as nine-year-old Melody and her cousin, Lonnie, discover artist Aunt Connie's new collection of portraits ready to be hung. The paintings "speak" to Melody and Lonnie, providing a powerful symbolic message about the reasons the children have to take pride in their identity as African Americans. This book is a vibrant lesson on the achievements of some remarkable historical figures.

Ringgold, Faith
Tar Beach
Crown Publishers, 1991
Ages 4-8, unpaged
ISBN 0-517-58030-6

Storyquilt artist Faith Ringgold created a unique wall hanging-cum-fictional narrative about a black child's flight of fancy while growing up in Harlem. This quilt is part of the collection of the Guggenheim Museum in New York City. In *Tar Beach*, each square of the quilt is accompanied by text that tells the story of eight-year-old Cassie Louise Lightfoot, who dreams of flying in the night sky above her apartment. As she circles over the flat tar roof of her building, Cassie imagines that she has claimed the sparkling jewel-like sights of Manhattan for her family, and that this will change some of the harsh realities of being poor and black in postwar America. Winner of the Coretta Scott King Award for children's illustration in 1992, a Caldecott Honor Book and a New York Times Best Illustrated Book.

In the sequel, *Aunt Harriet's Underground Railroad in the Sky* (Scholastic 1992: ISBN 0-517-58767), Cassie gets a bird's-eye view of the life of Underground Railroad conductor Harriet Tubman. After Cassie's imaginary flight, the book returns to earth to present a brief afterword on the "Black Moses," as Tubman was called, who made 19 trips south to rescue at least 300 slaves, including members of her own family.

Sadlier, Rosemary
Leading the Way: Black Women in Canada
Umbrella Press, 1994
Ages 12 and up, 72 pp.
ISBN 1-895642-11-6

Leading the Way highlights the achievements of five remarkable African-Canadian women. The profiles include Mary Ann Camberton Shadd (1823-1893), the first black woman publisher, Rosemary Brown (1930-), politician and social activist, and Carrie Best (1903-), the Nova Scotia journalist and broadcaster. Along with *Trials and Triumphs* (see page 15), this book is an excellent addition to middle and secondary school Canadian history studies and a fine source of information on events and figures young readers will encounter in novels about subjects such as the Underground Railroad.

San Souci, Robert D.
Sukey and the Mermaid
Illustrated by Brian Pinkney
Four Winds Press, 1992
Ages 4-9, unpaged
ISBN 0-02-778141-0

This retelling of a black American folktale features the hardworking Sukey, who struggles through her harsh life in a sagging South Carolina cabin under the stern gaze of her step-pa, Mister Jones. In a story reminiscent of a Cinderella tale, Sukey innocently discovers a beautiful brown-skinned mermaid who will grant her wishes for wealth and happiness. Although the plot takes some twists and turns for the worse, Sukey emerges triumphant over her *malafee* (mainland whiskey) drinking stepfather. In a poignant verse, Sukey's mother grieves over her ne'er-do-well lost husband—"Mister Jones wasn't much but he was all I had in this world." This gives readers an opening to explore beyond the pure good-versus-evil fairy tale motif. A Coretta Scott King Honor book in 1992.

Winter, Jeanette
Follow the Drinking Gourd
Knopf, 1988
Ages 5-9, 44 pp.
ISBN 0-394-89694-7

"When the sun comes back, and the first quail calls,
Follow the drinking gourd.
For the old man is a-waiting for to carry you to freedom
If you follow the drinking gourd."

   This sounds like a simple folk song sung by slaves, but it was actually a secret map to freedom. Hidden in the seemingly simple lyrics were directions for an escape route north to Canada—the Underground Railroad. Jeanette Winter tells the story of slaves Molly and James, torn apart when James is sold away to another master. An unassuming conductor on the Underground Railroad, Peg Leg Joe, leads the brave group of runaway slaves north to freedom in Canada. Included also is the music to the cryptic song, as well as some brief notes on the history of the Underground Railroad. This is an excellent introduction to the subject of slavery and freedom.

Woodson, Jacqueline
Last Summer with Maizon
Dell Yearling Paperbacks, 1992
Ages 10-14, 105 pp.
ISBN 0-440-40555-6

Margaret and Maizon (rhymes with "raisin") are best friends who live on the same Brooklyn street. But the summer they turn 11 is a time of upheaval in their lives. Margaret's father dies of a heart attack and, just when Margaret needs Maizon's presence, her exceptionally bright friend is awarded a scholarship to a competitive, elite private boarding school. This is a deftly written story of two urban black girls and their efforts to deal with the changing nature of relationships.

Readers will also enjoy the sequel, *Maizon at Blue Hill* (Delacorte Press, 1992: ISBN 0-385-30796-9), in which Maizon recounts her experiences being "black and smart" at an upscale Connecticut boarding school.

Yarbrough, Camille
Cornrows
Illustrated by Carole Byard
Coward-McCann, 1979
Ages 5-10, unpaged
ISBN 0-698-30750-X (hardcover)
      0-698-20709-2 (paperback—Sandcastle Books))

In Africa, the spirit of the people is represented in many different forms, such as sculpture, dance and ritual masquerade. Shirley Ann and her little brother, Me Too, appreciate the richness of their African heritage as it is expressed in the many patterns of braiding hair. Each tells a different story about the wearer. Information about the wearer's tribe, social caste, religion and more can be imparted through the number of braids, the direction of the swirls, the length of the braids, and the type and color of the beads and decorations.

While braiding Shirley Ann's hair, Mama and Great-Grammaw explain how the cornrows, a powerful African symbol since ancient times, can today symbolize the courage of outstanding figures in African-American history. Many African-American role models and leaders, such as Harriet Tubman, Marcus Garvey and Langston Hughes, are mentioned in the text. In this way, the book serves as an excellent springboard to discussion of and research into the lives of these individuals.

The Chinese Experience

Ashley, Bernard
Cleversticks
Illustrated by Derek Brazell
Picture Lions (HarperCollins), 1992
Ages 3-6, unpaged
ISBN 0-00-663855-4

After two days at his Kindergarten, Ling Sung is convinced that he never wants to go back again. He can't button up his jacket, and he doesn't know how to tie his shoelaces or write his name like the other kids do. When, in jest, he uses two paintbrushes as chopsticks to eat some biscuits, his teacher and classmates discover something special that Ling Sung can do better than anyone else. The colorful illustrations of the Kindergarten filled with a diverse throng of children busy at their activity centers provides a fresh and energetic backdrop to the story.

Levine, Ellen
I Hate English!
Illustrated by Steve Bjorkman
Scholastic, 1989
Ages 5-8, unpaged
ISBN 0-590-42305-3 (hardcover)
      0-590-42304-5 (paperback)

At her school in Hong Kong, Mei Mei was a star student who eagerly put up her hand to answer questions. At her new school in New York City, however, she understands most of what the teacher says, but never volunteers to speak because she can't get seem to get either her tongue or her mind around the strange new sounds and words of English. She stubbornly refuses to utter a word in her second language until a a caring and creative teacher helps her break down the barriers. Newcomers to an English-speaking society may recognize themselves in the pages of this story, while their North American-born friends will gain insights into the obstacles that must be overcome when learning to speak a new language in the midst of a new and strange culture.

Lim, Sing
West Coast Chinese Boy
Tundra Books, 1991
Ages 8 and up, 63 pp.
ISBN 0-88-776270-0

Artist Sing Lim's reminiscences of growing up in the 1920s on Pender Street in Vancouver's Chinatown are humorous and penetrating. Through a lively string of self-illustrated vignettes, Lim paints a fascinating picture of the cycle of life in the tenements along "Shanghai Alley." With wit and pathos, he describes ceremonies such as the traditional "baby's first head shave," which takes place at the age of one month, and the Moon Festival Bear Paw Feast, as well as the difficulties and prejudices he encountered growing up in an immigrant family.

Lord, Bette Bao
In the Year of the Boar and Jackie Robinson
HarperTrophy Paperbacks, 1986
Ages 8-12, 169 pp.
ISBN 0-06-440175-8

When her father sends for his wife and daughter to join him in post-war America, a 10-year-old Chinese girl excitedly takes the name of Shirley Temple Wong and sets sail for *mei guo*—the beautiful country. We laugh along with Shirley as she discovers wax candy lips and washing machines, practices blowing bubbles with her chewing gum and learns the morning speech at school—"I pledge a lesson to the frog of the United States of America." And our hearts go out to her when she longs for friends but finds the new Chinese girl at school hails from Chattanooga and speaks not a word of Chinese, or when she inadvertently interferes with the baseball trajectory of the biggest bully in the schoolyard and comes home with two black eyes. This incident opens Shirley's eyes to the wonderful American phenomenon of baseball. The first black player in the major leagues, Jackie Robinson, becomes a metaphor for Shirley's dogged progress toward adjusting to the ways of her new country. An American Library Association Notable Children's Book.

Namioka, Lensey
Yang the Youngest and his Terrible Ear
Illustrated by Kees de Kiefte
Dell Paperbacks, 1994
Ages 8-12, 134 pp.
ISBN 0-440-40917-9

The Yang family has just immigrated to Seattle, Washington. Like Mr. Yang, a symphony violinist, everyone in the family has a talent for music—except Yingtao, the youngest son. Yingtao's new best friend, Matthew, on the other hand, shows a real talent for the violin, to the annoyance of his father, who feels that his son is neglecting his athletic skills. Yingtao, however, shows a flair for baseball as soon as he picks up a bat. The story of how Yingtao and Matthew reconcile their respective talents with the aspirations of their parents forms the theme of this spirited novel, which is crammed with Yingtao's wry observations on his progress in adapting to life in America.

A sequel, *Yang the Third and Her Impossible Family* (Bantam Doubleday Dell, 1996: ISBN 0-440-41231-5), is now available in paperback.

Wallace, Ian
Chin Chiang and the Dragon's Dance
Douglas & McIntyre, 1984
Ages 4-9, unpaged
ISBN 0-88899-020-2

Although he has always dreamed of being old enough to participate in the New Year's dragon dance, Chin Chiang is stricken with stage fright when the great moment finally arrives. He is afraid he will stumble, disgrace his family and bring misfortune upon them all. Wanting to be alone, Chin Chiang takes refuge on the roof of the public library, where he meets the elderly cleaning lady, Pu Yee. The old woman helps Chin Chiang regain his confidence and he goes on to be a proud and spirited dragon's tail in the colorful Vancouver parade. The illustrations in this picture book are splendid, with finely detailed images of the festivities glowing in the red that signifies good fortune.

Two excellent non-fiction resources that complement this book are *Lion Dancer: Ernie Wan's Chinese New Year* (Scholastic, 1990: ISBN 0-590-43047-5) by Kate Waters and Madeline Slovenz Low, a photographic essay of Ernie's first lion dance in New York's Chinatown, and Tricia Brown's *Chinese New Year* (Henry Holt, 1987: ISBN 0-8050-0497-1), a record in black-and-white snapshots of San Francisco's Chinese New Year traditions and celebrations.

Yee, Paul
Roses Sing on New Snow
Illustrated by Harvey Chan
Groundwood Books, 1991
Ages 4-8, unpaged
ISBN 0-88899-144-4

In Vancouver's Chinatown at the turn of the century, Maylin slaves all day in a hot kitchen creating delectable dishes to serve to the customers in her father's restaurant. Although the restaurant has garnered an excellent reputation for its cuisine, Maylin's father doesn't want anyone to know that a woman creates the wondrous dishes. He keeps the kitchen door shut tight and tells everyone that it is his two sons who are the expert chefs. When the visiting governor of South China comes to dine at the restaurant, however, Maylin turns circumstances to her own advantage, revealing the identity of the chef and receiving the praise she so richly deserves. Harvey Chan's colorful illustrations of richly laden tables are mouth-watering in their own right.

Yep, Laurence
The Star Fisher
Puffin Paperbacks, 1991
Ages 10-14, 150 pp.
ISBN 0-14-036003-4

When 16-year-old Joan Lee and her family move from Ohio to smalltown West Virginia to establish a small laundry business, they are in for a mixed reception from the townspeople. An especially effective device in this adolescent novel is the use of italics to highlight dialogue in English and a roman font for conversations in Chinese, the language in which the family feels most comfortable. Joan's struggle to keep her unique cultural identity while integrating into American society is the basis for a satisfying, well-written novel.

The European Experience

Bartone, Elisa
Peppe the Lamplighter
Illustrated by Ted Lewin
Lothrop, Lee & Shepard, 1993
Ages 5-10, unpaged
ISBN 0-688-10268-9

In turn-of-the-century New York City, Peppe lives in a Little Italy tenement with his large, poor family. Because his father is ill, Peppe must work to help support his sisters and send money to family members still in Italy. The only job he can find is lighting the gas lamps on the dark, crowded streets. At first, Peppe enjoys the job, imagining that he is in church lighting candles to the saints. But his father is ashamed that his son is a lamplighter and discourages Peppe's pride in his work—until his younger daughter is lost on the dark streets. Then, lighting the lamps becomes "the best job in America." Although the story is more than a little melodramatic, the illustrations provide a wonderful glimpse of life in another era. A Caldecott Honor Book in 1994.

Bonners, Susan
The Wooden Doll
Lothrop, Lee & Shepard, 1991
Ages 4-8, unpaged
ISBN 0-688-08280-7

On a visit to her Polish grandparents' home, Stephanie itches to play with her grandfather's brightly painted, old wooden doll, which remains tantalizingly out of reach atop Grandma's china cabinet. One day, when no one is looking, Stephanie climbs up on a chair and brings the doll down. She discovers that it hides a marvelous secret: inside is nested a whole family of smaller and smaller identical dolls. But the doll also holds another secret: on its bottom is written "Stephania," the special name that only her grandpa calls her. In unraveling the mystery, Stephanie finds that the snugly fitting matrushka dolls contain a special link with her past. Juanita Havill's *Treasure Nap* (see page 37), another book on a similar theme, is an excellent companion to *The Wooden Doll*.

Polacco, Patricia
Just Plain Fancy
Bantam Books, 1990
Ages 4-8, unpaged
ISBN 0-553-05884-3

Naomi, an Amish girl living in the fertile farm country of Pennsylvania, adheres to the simple ways of her people, which have been impressed upon her by her parents and elders of the community. One day, she and her sister, Ruth, find an abandoned egg in the tall grass near their henhouse. Naomi keeps the egg warm but, when the chick hatches, she is terrified that it is much too fancy to suit the modest lifestyle of her people. Polacco's book is a warm and sympathetic portrayal of a group about which many children know very little.

An excellent non-fiction accompaniment to this story is Raymond Bial's *Amish Home* (Houghton Mifflin, 1993: ISBN 0-395-59504-5). Bial's photographic study includes only pictures of objects in the Amish home and their surroundings, never any Amish folk whose beliefs prevent them from being photographed. Clear text outlines the simplicity and purpose of the Amish way of life.

Wallace, Ian & Angela Wood
The Sandwich
Kids Can Press, 1975
Ages 6-10, unpaged
ISBN 0-919964-02-8

Vincenzo Ferrante lives with his family above a variety store in downtown Toronto. When his grandmother must go into the hospital, Vincenzo has to start taking his lunch to school in a bag rather than returning home for a hot meal. Together, he and his father prepare one of Vincenzo's favorite sandwiches—mortadella and provolone on crusty, fresh bread. But when he unwraps his sandwich in the school cafeteria, Vincenzo's friends—looking up from their peanut butter on white bread—make fun of it, saying that it smells like dead socks. Primary grade learners will enjoy finding out how Vincenzo resolves his problem of feeling different from the other children without joining them in taking peanut butter sandwiches for lunch. A Canadian Children's Book Centre "Our Choice" selection.

Winter, Jeanette
Klara's New World
Knopf, 1992
Ages 5-10, unpaged
ISBN 0-679-80626-1

Klara's family is struggling to make a good life in Sweden but, if their fortunes don't improve, they will have to hire out eight-year-old Klara as a chore girl. Then, a friend writes from America, describing a land that is very different. When Klara's parents decide to emigrate, she knows it will mean leaving behind everything she has ever known—her home, her village and her beloved grandfather. In this jewel-toned picture book, author-illustrator Jeanette Winter tells of a journey undertaken by millions during the great wave of immigration to the United States in the late 19th and early 20th centuries. Based on the letters and diaries of Scandinavian immigrants, the book filters their experiences through the eyes of a child. An afterword supplies historical background to the period.

Zucker, David
Uncle Carmello
Illustrated by Lyle Miller
Macmillan, 1993
Ages 5-8, unpaged
ISBN 0-02-793760-7

When David visits Uncle Carmello for the first time, it seems that all the stories about his gruffness are true. Uncle Carmello won't let David play on the junk-filled porch, explore the overgrown backyard, or play ship's captain at the old wooden wheel in the mysterious cellar. What's more, David can't understand his uncle's heavily accented English. But one day, when David's mother leaves him alone with his uncle, the two go on a shopping trip to Boston's Italian neighborhood where another side of Uncle Carmello is revealed. The detailed watercolor illustrations of street life in Boston's Little Italy are a strong point of this book, which deals very well with the sometimes strained beginnings of a rewarding intergenerational relationship.

The Hispanic Experience

Atkin, S. Beth
Voices from the Fields: Children of Migrant Farmworkers Tell Their Stories
Little, Brown, 1993
Ages 12 and up, 96 pp.
ISBN 0-316-05633-2

Evocative photographs, candid first-person interviews and poems in Spanish and English are woven together in this book that offers readers a glimpse of what life is like for the children of contemporary migrant workers. In their own words, the nine children interviewed, ranging in age from nine to 18, explain what it's like to live a life of hardship in a country as rich as the United States. But these young people also speak of their pride in their Mexican heritage and of the strong bonds that unite members of their families. All passionately express their aspirations for a better and more stable life. *Voices from the Fields* provides a powerful historical record of the Hispanic migrant experience in America through the eyes of its young people.

Buss, Fran Leeper, assisted by Daisy Cubias
Journey of the Sparrows
Lodestar/Dutton Books, 1991
Ages 10-14, 155 pp.
ISBN 0-525-67362-8 (hardcover)
    0-440-40785-0 (paperback—Dell/Yearling)

Nailed inside a crate on the back of a produce truck, 15-year-old Maria, her little brother, Oscar, and pregnant older sister, Julia, endure a terrifying flight across the Mexican border after both their father and Julia's husband are assassinated because of their involvement in political activities in their homeland of El Salvador. Arriving in Chicago, they join the invisible mass of "illegal aliens" trying desperately to survive while living in constant fear of discovery and deportation by the authorities. To ensure the authenticity of this story, Fran Leeper Buss enlisted the assistance of Salvadoran refugee Daisy Cubias.

    Another novel that depicts the ordeals of illegal immigrants to the U.S. is Patricia Beatty's *Lupita Mañana* (Beech Tree Paperbacks, 1992: ISBN 0-688-

11497-0). Originally published in 1981, the story outlines the harsh realities facing immigrants who lack education and skills.

Cisneros, Sandra
Hairs—Pelitos
Illustrated by Terry Ybáñez
Knopf, 1994
Ages 4-8, unpaged
ISBN 0-679-86171-8

Taken from Sandra Cisneros' 1984 book, *The House on Mango Street*, this lovely short poem is presented in both English and Spanish. The young narrator describes the unique qualities of each member of her family in terms of their hair. Especially touching is her description of burrowing in her mother's hair, which she compares to the smell of warm, freshly baked bread. Every child will identify with the cozy and safe feelings evoked when she describes snuggling in bed basking in the smell of Mama's warm hair, as Papa snores and rain drums on the windowpanes. An excellent read-aloud for younger children, this book can also become a springboard to creative writing with students in the junior grades.

Dawson, Mildred Leinweber
Over Here It's Different: Carolina's Story
Photographed by George Ancona
Macmillan, 1993
Ages 8-12, unpaged
ISBN 0-02-726328-2

During the 1980s, more than 250,000 people from the Dominican Republic made a new home in the mainland United States. In *Over Here It's Different*, the author tells the story of one of these immigrants, 11-year-old Carolina Liranzo, who moved to New York City at the age of seven. As well as sketching a sympathetic portrait of life in America through Carolina's eyes, the author shows some of the complexities and red-tape involved in immigrating to the U.S. While the tone occasionally lapses into dryness, the book is filled with information about life in the Dominican Republic and examples of the melding of immigrant and American cultures.

Dorros, Arthur
Radio Man: A Story in English and Spanish
Spanish translation by Sandra Marulanda Dorros
HarperCollins, 1993
Ages 6-10, unpaged
ISBN 0-06-021547-X

Diego and his family are migrant farm workers. Their truck takes them from Texas to Arizona to California following the harvests of the cabbage, melon and cherry crops. Each temporary stop may bring Diego new friends or reunite him with old ones but, no matter where he goes, Diego always keeps one thing with him—his radio. The voices on the radio remind him of the places he has been, help him learn about the places he is heading toward, and keep him in touch with the people he meets. This bilingual book paints a simple and non-judgmental picture of the life of migrant children in the United States.

Dorros, Arthur
Abuela
Illustrated by Elisa Kleven
Dutton Children's Books, 1991
Ages 4-8, unpaged
ISBN 0-525-44750-4

Every child dreams of being able to fly. In this adventure story, Rosalba travels with her grandmother to the park to feed the birds and enjoy the scenery. While scattering crumbs, Rosalba suddenly imagines what it would be like to soar high above the park and look down on the city. She calls Abuela up to join her and together they sail on a marvelous journey over Manhattan. Many of the sights they see have a special significance for Rosalba's *abuela*, reminding her of her own arrival in a new country. Rosalba's English narrative is spiced with many Spanish phrases, which add another strong link between the generations. Elisa Kleven's artwork is truly glorious, packed with childlike details that illuminate the city scenes in a patchwork of brilliant colors. *Abuela* is a beautiful story about the bond of love and shared cultural pride between a little girl and her treasured grandmother.

Garza, Carmen Lomas
Family Pictures/Cuadros de Familia
Children's Book Press, 1990
Ages 4-8, 32 pp.
ISBN 0-89239-050-6

Carmen Lomas Garza is considered one of the major Mexican-American painters in the United States today. *Family Pictures* is the result of her reminiscences, in painting and words, of her childhood growing up in a traditional Hispanic community in south Texas. Illustrated in a vibrant and childlike style, the bilingual English-Spanish text recalls the everyday activities that meant so much to the artist—picking oranges or nopal cactus with her grandparents and watching her grandmother slaughter a squawking chicken for a pleasurable Sunday dinner. Special occasions such as a trip to a Mexican fair, a birthday party and a candlelit Christmas pageant are also lovingly remembered.

Gordon, Ginger
My Two Worlds
Photographed by Martha Cooper
Clarion Books, 1993
Ages 5-8, unpaged
ISBN 0-395-58704-2

Follow Kirsy Rodriguez, a Hispanic-American eight-year-old, as she journeys to her family's hometown in the Dominican Republic for the Christmas holidays. Kirsy spends her vacations with her grandparents and friend in Puerto Plata. Although readers get glimpses of children's everyday lives at play and helping out with chores, we do not see them at school or in their homes, which is a drawback to this book. Kirsy sums ups her dual identity by saying, "Sometimes I wonder if I'd rather live in the Dominican Republic instead of New York City...I'm glad I don't have to choose—I belong to both worlds and each is a part of me." While Kirsy's experiences need to be balanced in the classroom with those of refugee children who have no choices, this book makes a good catalyst for discussing how it feels to be torn between allegiances to two countries.

Havill, Juanita
Treasure Nap
Illustrated by Elivia Savadier
Houghton Mifflin, 1992
Ages 4-8, unpaged
ISBN 0-395-57817-5

On a stifling afternoon when it is too hot even to nap, Alicia asks to hear, for the umpteenth time, the story of how her great-great-grandmother came from Mexico to the United States. So Mama comfortably settles back and slips into the tale of a long-ago little girl who traveled up into the mountains of Mexico to bid goodbye to her grandfather, and left his village with a special treasure to help her remember him forever. Lulled to sleep, Alicia awakes when it is cooler, and extracts all Great-Great-Grandmother's treasures from the wicker basket where they are kept. This charming image of continuity and family folklore in a Mexican-American family may encourage children to explore their own family stories and backgrounds.

Howlett, Bud
I'm New Here
Houghton Mifflin, 1993
Ages 6-12, 32 pp.
ISBN 0-395-64049-0

Newly arrived from El Salvador, Jazmin Escalante is nervous about what awaits her on her first day at her new Miami school. Because of the civil strife in her homeland, Jazmin did not attend fourth grade in El Salvador, so it is decided to place her there, even though she should be in Grade 5. Making no attempt to determine the correct Spanish pronunciation of her name, the teacher introduces Jazmin to the class and presents her with a box of crayons for coloring pictures. At home, that night, Jazmin is discouraged about the way her American school career is beginning. But with the arrival of Mrs. Diaz, the bilingual English as a second language teacher who will instruct her for an hour and a half each day, things begin to fall into place. After she's tested in Spanish in math and reading, Jazmin is moved into Grade 5, begins to make friends and, as she says happily on the last page of the book, "I didn't feel like I was new here anymore."

Bud Howlett's simple, empathetic portrayal of a likable young girl and her family as they adjust to a new society and language should be required reading for every school child—and classroom teacher.

Mikaelson, Ben
Sparrow Hawk Red
Hyperion Books, 1993
Ages 10-14, 185 pp.
ISBN 1-56282-387-6

When his father, an ex-drug enforcement agent, is visited by some former associates, 13-year-old Ricky Diaz finds out the truth about his mother's death: she was murdered. This revelation inspires Ricky to try to complete the mission his father could not: to steal back an American-made radar detector installed in a single-engine plane used by drug dealers to smuggle narcotics into the United States from Mexico. Once in Mexico, Ricky blends in with the *rateros*, the homeless street children, and, barely surviving from hunger, meets Sledad, a *ratera* who becomes a useful ally—and close friend. This book will appeal to fans of Hardy Boys-style mysteries, while teaching them about the difficult life faced by the homeless in Mexico.

Mora, Pat
Listen to the Desert/Oye al Desierto
Illustrated by Francisco X. Mora
Clarion Books, 1994
Ages 3-6, unpaged
ISBN 0-395-67292-9

This bilingual sound poem in Spanish and English describes some of the noises made by animals and the forces of nature in the desert of the southwestern United States. Young children will enjoy the onomatopoeic verses and comparing the Spanish and English representations of the calls of animals such as the owl, coyote, toad and dove.

Soto, Gary
Baseball in April and Other Stories
Odyssey/Harcourt Brace, 1990
Ages 10-14, 157 pp.
ISBN 0-15-205720-X (hardcover)
0-15-205721-8 (paperback)

The 11 short stories in this collection focus on the everyday adventures of Hispanic young people growing up in Fresno, California. Their charm lies in author Gary Soto's talent for making such seemingly banal events as sitting in seventh grade French class or a Saturday afternoon cruise around the mall resonate with the bittersweetness of adolescent experiences everywhere. There is, for example, the story of Manuel, who volunteers to lipsynch Richie Valens' classic hit "La Bamba" at the school talent show, only to have the needle on the record player stick. And there is seventh-grader Michael, who has learned over the summer that girls are attracted to a fierce scowl, which he practices at every opportunity, as well as Maria, who announces that she is too mature to accompany her family on the annual car trip, only to spend the entire vacation worrying that her parents and brothers have been involved in a fatal car accident. A glossary helps readers understand the slang and Spanish expressions sprinkled throughout the wry dialogue. This appealing collection works well as a read-aloud or for independent reading.

Soto, Gary
Too Many Tamales
Putnam, 1993
Ages 4-8, unpaged
ISBN 0-399-22146-8

Adults who chuckled through the adventures of Homer Price in their childhood will remember Homer's peccadillo with a gold bracelet and his inventor uncle's amazing donut-making machine. In this book, Gary Soto adds a Hispanic twist to this tried-and-true plot, as young Maria absentmindedly plays with her mother's diamond ring while stirring a big bowl of *tamale* corn meal mixture. After much embarrassment and a few severe cases of upset stomach, the missing ring is located and the family can get back to celebrating the Christmas season with appropriate gusto.

Thomas, Jane Resh
Lights on the River
Illustrated by Michael Dooling
Hyperion Books, 1994
Ages 4-8, unpaged
ISBN 0-7868-0004-6

As Teresa and her family travel around the United States eking out a meager living as migrant farmworkers, home is a succession of tumbledown huts and former chicken coops. The family follows the ripening crops of cucumbers, peaches and sugar beets around the land in their cramped station wagon, often enduring substandard housing conditions and poor pay in their efforts to support themselves and family members in Mexico. Teresa and her family are pragmatic about their lifestyle, which gives the story an authentic feel. Because one of the themes is Teresa's memory of launching lighted candles along the river during her Mexican village's Christmas festivities, this book can be integrated into a winter holiday unit. It also works well in a unit on housing or different kinds of work.

In a brief afterword, author Jane Resh Thomas points out that people of Hispanic descent do every kind of work in the United States today, from serving in the President's Cabinet to providing a significant proportion of the migrant workforce that supplies farm labor. A fine choice to pair with Arthur Dorros' *Radio Man: A Story in English and Spanish* (see page 35).

The Japanese Experience

Irwin, Hadley
Kim/Kimi
Puffin Paperbacks, 1987
Ages 12-16, 200 pp.
ISBN 0-14-50428-4

Kim Andrews, born Kimi Yogushi, is 16 years old and searching for answers about her Japanese American father who died before she was born. Even the warm and loving family life she has with her mother, stepfather and half-brother can't keep her from feeling that she is not all of a piece. When Kim embarks on a trip that takes her from her home in a suburban Iowa community to the site of one of the camps where Japanese Americans were incarcerated during World War II, she finally confronts her father's past and her own future.

Kogawa, Joy
Naomi's Road
Oxford University Press, 1988
Ages 9-12, 82 pp.
ISBN 0-19-540547-1

When Naomi Nakane is five years old in 1942, her happy family life in Vancouver is torn apart by the forced relocation of Japanese Canadians to internment camps in the interior of British Columbia. The story follows Naomi and her family through the war years as they are separated and forced to deal with deprivation and prejudice. Yet Naomi emerges with a spirit of hope and understanding that things can be better.

A children's version of *Obasan*, Joy Kogawa's award-winning novel for adult readers, *Naomi's Road* explores a difficult and bitter episode in Canadian history. Yoshiko Uchida's *Journey to Topaz* (Aladdin Paperbacks, 1992: ISBN 0-689-71641-9) is another good book for the same age group dealing with the internment of Japanese Americans in the western desert of the United States.

Means, Florence Crannell
The Moved-Outers
Walker and Company, 1945 (Re-issued 1992)
Ages 12-16, 156 pp.
ISBN 0-8027-7386-9 (paperback)

Another moving story of life in the Japanese internment camps is Florence Crannell Means' *The Moved-Outers*. A Newbery Honor book in 1946, the story is still fresh and relevant today. Sue Ohara and her family have always thought of themselves as Americans. But after the December 7, 1941, attack by Japan on Pearl Harbor, they suddenly become "Japanese." Relocated to a series of incarceration camps, 18-year-old Sue and her family try not only to survive but also to remain loyal Americans.

Mochizuki, Ken
Baseball Saved Us
Illustrated by Dom Lee
Lee and Low Books, 1993
Ages 5-10, 32 pp.
ISBN 1-880000-01-6

Inside the barbed-wire fences of a Japanese internment camp in the American West during World War II, the detainees need a positive focus for their attention. So the entire camp population pitches in to construct a baseball diamond, build the bleachers, sew the uniforms and coach the young players. Based on an actual event, this moving story shows how the baseball games not only united the detainees, but also helped build the confidence of a young boy named Shorty. It is particularly ironic that these Americans, stripped of their freedom, citizenship and worldly possessions, fall back on the "all-American" image of baseball to get them through the toughest times.

Momiji Health Care Society
Baachan! Geechan! Arigato
Momiji Health Care Society, 1989
Ages 8-12, unpaged
ISBN 0-9693867-0-2

By following the lives of the members of one family who were shipped to labor and internment camps during World War II, this book recounts the history of

Japanese Canadians. Although the injustices they suffered during the war are the centerpiece of the story, the book also describes the good life they lived before the war and how they rebuilt their lives when they were released from the camps. It culminates with the signing of the Japanese Canadian Redress Agreement in 1988, which embodied a formal apology and restitution for those whose lives had been affected during the war, enabling them to close the door on this sad chapter in their past. The book includes a useful chronology of events in Canadian history with particular significance for Japanese Canadians.

Say, Allen
Grandfather's Journey
Houghton Mifflin, 1993
Ages 5-10, 32 pp.
ISBN 0-395-57035-2

"The funny thing is, the moment I am in one country I am homesick for the other." These are the words of the grandfather of Allen Say, the renowned Japanese-American author and illustrator. Journeying to the United States as a young man, Say's grandfather is fascinated and excited by the changing American landscape as well as by the endless parade of new and interesting people. He finally settles permanently in California but, many years later, he is stricken with a longing to be in his homeland once again and returns to Japan where his daughter marries and his grandson is born. Decades later, Say, the grandson, embarks on a similar journey of self-discovery to the United States. The feelings of being torn by a love for two countries are thus poignantly expressed across the generations. Among the many accolades and awards gathered by this beautifully written and illustrated book is the Caldecott Medal.

Uchida, Yoshiko
The Bracelet
Illustrated by Joanna Yardley
Philomel Books, 1993
Ages 6-10, unpaged
ISBN 0-399-22503-X

Drawing upon her own childhood in the United States during World War II, author Yoshiko Uchida tells the poignant tale of how seven-year-old Emi's childhood is affected by a war she doesn't even understand. The year is 1942, and the American government is forcing Emi and her family to move to an internment camp because of their Japanese heritage. As they prepare to depart, Emi's best friend, Laurie, gives her a farewell gift—a thin gold bracelet with a heart dangling from it. When Emi loses the treasured bracelet in the cold and desolate camp, she learns that nothing can take away the memories and the love that is in her heart. Uchida's sensitive treatment of this tragic period in American history combined with Joanna Yardley's watercolor illustrations, which beautifully evoke the waning and reawakening of Emi's hopes, earned this book a place on the *New York Times* list of best-illustrated books of 1993.

Uchida, Yoshiko
A Jar of Dreams
Macmillan/Aladdin Paperbacks, 1981
Ages 9-12, 131 pp.
ISBN 0-689-71041-0

Growing up in Depression-era California, 11-year-old Rinko wants to be like any other American girl. But prejudice rears its ugly head in the form of Wilbur Starr, the owner of a neighborhood laundry. Starr holds a stereotypical view of Japanese immigrants, which comes to the fore when Rinko's family opens a laundering business that competes with his. Through the wise influence of her visiting Aunt Waka from Japan, Rinko learns to look past the intolerance and become proud of her Japanese heritage.

Readers will also enjoy the other two volumes in the Rinko trilogy: *The Best Bad Thing* (Macmillan/Aladdin, 1983: ISBN 0-689-71745-8) and *The Happiest Ending* (M.K. McElderry, 1985: 0-689-50326-1).

The Korean Experience

Choi, Sook Nyul
Halmoni and the Picnic
Illustrated by Karen M. Dugan
Houghton Mifflin, 1993
Ages 5-8, unpaged
ISBN 0-395-61626-3

Yunmi's grandmother, Halmoni, has just moved to New York City from Korea, and is finding it difficult to adjust to American life. The customs are very different; for example, she can't get used to the way Yunmi cheerfully calls out a hello to her adult neighbors instead of lowering her eyes in respect. Though she was a teacher in Korea and knows some English, she is embarrassed to speak it because of her accent. To help Halmoni adjust, Yunmi and her friends devise a way of including her on a class trip to Central Park, which finally enables her to begin to feel a part of life in America. Sensitive, richly colored drawings illustrate this warm, intergenerational story and evoke the close relationship between Yunmi and her grandmother.

Girard, Linda Walvoord
We Adopted You, Benjamin Koo
Illustrated by Linda Shute
Albert Whitman, 1989
Ages 6-10, unpaged
ISBN 0-8075-8694-3 (hardcover)
    0-8075-8695-1 (paperback)

Soon after Benjamin Koo Andrews' birth mother left him on the doorstep of a Korean orphanage, he was adopted by American parents of European descent and taken to the United States. Nine-year-old Benjamin recounts the changes he went through once he was old enough to realize he was different: how he came to accept that he doesn't look at all like anyone else in his family and won't ever be able to find out about his birth mother. His encounters with sympathetic teachers and friends, as well as the way he deals with remarks by children and well-meaning, but ignorant, strangers are skilfully handled. This book compassionately portrays a subject that some children may have difficulty dealing with.

Kline, Suzy
Song Lee in Room 2B
Illustrated by Frank Remkiewicz
Viking, 1993
Ages 7-10, 56 pp.
ISBN 0-670-84772-0

Song Lee, the shy second grader in Miss Mackle's Room 2B, is still perfecting her English. So, when called upon to give a talk about her favorite vacation spot, she dresses up as a cherry tree by covering herself with dozens of pink Kleenex blossoms and has the tree take the class on a tour of Seoul, Korea. Other adventures occur when she brings her pet salamander, Chungju, to school and when a huge lump of green clay ends up on the top of her head during the class's St. Patrick's Day party. This sprightly early chapter book will inspire chuckles from young readers.

Lee, Marie G.
If It Hadn't Been for Yoon Jun
Houghton Mifflin, 1993
Ages 10-14, 134 pp.
ISBN 0-395-62941-1

Alice Larsen, adopted as an infant, is the first Korean immigrant to attend her small-town Minnesota junior high school. Alice considers herself thoroughly American, but when Yoon Jun, a new arrival from Korea, arrives at the school, she is compelled to confront her Korean heritage. An entertaining read for middle school students, this book adds a new twist to the classic theme of an adolescent's search for popularity and acceptance.

Lee, Marie G.
Finding My Voice
Houghton Mifflin, 1993
Ages 12-16, 165 pp.
ISBN 0-395-62134-8 (hardcover)
     0-440-021896-9 (paperback—Dell)

Rushing through her morning makeup regimen, putting on eye shadow according to *Glamour* magazine's advice on giving depth to Oriental eyes, Ellen Sung prepares for the first day of her senior year at high school. The only Asian student in her small school,

Ellen determinedly ignores a boy on the bus who calls her a chink. Maybe someday I'll stop to really think about it, about what it means to be different, she thinks. But the stress of events in her final year, the pressure from her traditional Korean family for her to achieve top marks in order to be admitted to Harvard, and her new relationship with a popular, handsome, non-Asian school football hero all cause her to confront the fact that she is different. This snappily written first novel was chosen as an American Library Association Best Book for Young Adults.

Look for the sequel, *Saying Goodbye* (Houghton Mifflin, 1994; ISBN 0-395-67066-7), in which Ellen continues to meet the challenges of finding her identity as she travels to the east coast to enter Harvard.

Paek, Min
Aekyung's Dream
Children's Book Press, 1988
Ages 6-10, 24 pp.
ISBN 0-89239-042-5

In Korea, Aekyung used to awaken with enthusiasm for the day ahead. But after six months in America, she doesn't even feel like getting out of bed. English is still very difficult for her and her schoolmates tease her about her "Chinese" eyes, not even knowing the difference between Korea and China. One night, Aekyung dreams that she has traveled back in time to the magnificent 15th-century palace of King Sejong of Korea. As the court dancers gather around her, the wise ruler encourages Aekyung to be strong "like a tree with deep roots." Keeping this advice in mind after she wakes, Aekyung redoubles her efforts to learn English and adjust to her new surroundings, and she is finally rewarded with the acceptance and admiration of her peers. The simple English text is accompanied by a full Korean translation.

The South Asian Experience

Gilmore, Rachna
Lights for Gita
Illustrated by Alice Priestly
Second Story Press, 1994
Ages 4-8, unpaged
ISBN 0-929005-61-9 (paperback)

As members of Gita's family prepare to celebrate their first Divali festival in their new Canadian home, her hopes for a special celebration with her new friends are dashed when the wet November evening brings freezing rain and a power blackout. Of course, Gita overcomes her disappointment and finds the special meaning of the holiday in her heart. Although the ending is clichéd, this is one of the only appealing picture books that integrates the Hindu festival of Divali into a North American context and, as a result, is useful for educators of children in the early grades.

Perkins, Mitali
The Sunita Experiment
Hyperion Paperbacks, 1994
Ages 10-14, 179 pp.
ISBN 1-56282-671-9

When her very traditional grandparents come for a visit from India to California, 13-year-old Sunita Sen's mother suddenly trades in her jeans for flowing saris, and spicy curries replace pizza at the family dinner table. Sunita finds herself resenting her Indian heritage and embarrassed by the differences she feels between herself and her friends. She feels like a guinea pig in some kind of "experiment" to see what will emerge when some parts Indian and some parts American culture are thrown together. This is a funny and well-written novel of cultural double identity.

Rana, Indi
The Roller Birds of Rampur
Fawcett/Juniper Paperbacks, 1994
Ages 12 and up, 298 pp.
ISBN 0-8050-2670-3 (hardcover)

Seventeen-year-old Sheila Mehta's childhood friend, Munnia, is about to get married in India and accepts things just the way they are. Not so Sheila. Angry at her English boyfriend for rejecting her, at her parents for taking her to a country where people look down on those with brown skins, and at her homeland, India, for its dirt and poverty, Sheila can't accept anything the way it is. Her trip to India from England for Munnia's wedding, however, becomes the catalyst that helps Sheila start piecing together her identity.

Stone, Susheila
Nadeem Makes Samosas
Photographs by Chris Fairclough
Evans Brothers, 1987
Ages 4-8, 26 pp.
ISBN 0-237-60155-9

This is one of a series of books produced in England that depict life for children and families of the British South Asian community. Each book contains bilingual text in English and one of the major South Asian languages—Bengali, Punjabi or Urdu. In *Nadeem Makes Samosas*, a young boy accompanies his mother on a shopping trip to purchase the ingredients for samosas, then he and his mother prepare the succulent vegetable-filled pastries. The simple text is accompanied by realistic photographs that show Nadeem and the family in the context of their home life. If children's appetites are whetted by this mouth-watering photo essay, a recipe for samosas follows the story. Other titles in the series are *Manzur Goes to the Airport* (English-Bengali: ISBN 0-237-60159-1) and *Ranjit and the Fire Engines* (English-Punjabi: ISBN 0-237-60156-7).

The Southeast Asian Experience

Ashabranner, Brent & Melissa Ashabranner
Into a Strange Land: Unaccompanied Refugee Youth in America
Putnam, 1987
Ages 10 and up, 120 pp.
ISBN 0-399-21709-6

Among the millions of political refugees who have arrived in the United States over the past two decades are many thousands of young children and teenagers who have lost their families. *Into a Strange Land* tells the stories of some of these young, vulnerable refugees from Southeast Asia and the many caring American foster families that are helping them build new lives. Realistically and sympathetically, the father-daughter author team covers issues such as depression and the difficulties of adjusting to life in a foster family or group home. This book is liberally illustrated with photographs of the young refugees.

Bell, William
Absolutely Invincible
General Paperbacks, 1991
Ages 12 and up, 198 pp.
ISBN 0-7736-7291-5

Though very bright as well as highly skilled in the martial arts, 15-year-old George Ma is crippled by amnesia, the result of a horror-filled escape from the ravages of war in his native Southeast Asian country. At his Canadian high school, George befriends three other young people with disabilities, forging an alliance they dub "The Cripples' Club." The support of his friends acts as a catalyst for George to begin slowly piecing together his past. This is an appealing adolescent story with a sensitivity that belies the rather hard-edged writing style.

Crew, Linda
Children of the River
Dell Paperbacks, 1991
Ages 12 and up, 213 pp.
ISBN 0-440-21022-4

Cambodian teenager Sundara Sovann managed to flee her homeland after it was ravaged by the Khmer Rouge. Now, four years later, she is 17 and living in Oregon with her aunt's family, determined to find out whether her parents, brother and sister are alive. While she yearns to be accepted at her high school, she also wants to continue to adhere to her traditional Cambodian family values. Drawn into a friendship with Jonathan, a sensitive American boy who empathizes with her situation, Sundara finds that the relationship is blossoming into something more. Her struggle to reconcile her deepening feelings for Jonathan with her culture's traditional views on the inappropriateness of young people making their own romantic choices forms the crux of this well-written young adult novel.

Garland, Sherry
The Lotus Seed
Illustrated by Tatsuro Kiuchi
Harcourt Brace Jovanovich, 1993
Ages 6-12, unpaged
ISBN 0-15-249465-0

Lustrous oil paintings provide a rich counterpoint to Sherry Garland's spare narrative about the flight of a family to the United States from their native Vietnam. Through devastating civil war, the perilous voyage by boat to freedom, and the family's new life in a strange new land, the grandmother guards the one precious memento she has been able to salvage from her life in Vietnam, a lotus seed picked from the Imperial garden before the Emperor abdicated his throne to pave the way for the country's independence. One day, her small grandson finds the seed and plants it in a mud patch by their house. The flowering of the lotus seed lyrically parallels the experience of members of this refugee family in adjusting to a new way of life while trying to preserve their own special cultural heritage.

Gilson, Jamie
Hello, My Name Is Scrambled Eggs
Minstrel Books, 1986
Ages 9-14, 160 pp.
ISBN 0-671-74104-7

Seventh-grader Harvey Trumble's family makes room in their home and their hearts for a Vietnamese refugee family sponsored by their church. Harvey takes on the mission of helping their son, Tuan, adapt to American society, from teaching him expressions like Wow! and No kidding!, to instructing him on the coolest jeans to wear and drilling him in how to shoot marbles. In the end, of course, Harvey and his gang have a few things to learn about fitting in from Tuan. This book is a fast-paced and jaunty read with a pleasantly delivered message for the Grade 4-8 set.

Goldfarb, Mace
Fighters, Refugees, Immigrants: A Story of the Hmong
Carolrhoda Books, 1982
Ages 8 and up, 48 pp.
ISBN 0-87614-197-1

Because the tribespeople of mountainous northern Laos, known as the Hmong, formed an alliance with the United States during the Vietnam conflict, they were persecuted after the downfall of the American-backed Laotian government. As a result, tens of thousands of Hmong fled over the mountains and across the Mekong River to Thailand—and many met their deaths on the treacherous journey. Mace Goldfarb, an American pediatrician who volunteered to serve as a doctor in a Hmong refugee camp just inside the Thai border, documents life in the camp, especially among the children. The text is supported by haunting photographs of war-ravaged Hmong children and their families whose strength and optimism nevertheless shine through as they turn their faces to the camera.

Surat, Michele Maria
Angel Child, Dragon Child
Illustrated by Vo-Dinh Mai
Scholastic, 1989
Ages 5-8, 38 pp.
ISBN 0-590-42271-5 (paperback)

Nguyen Hoa, who prefers to be called Ut—"a tender name for smallest daughter"—has just immigrated to the United States from Vietnam, and doesn't like her new American school. The children all laugh when she speaks Vietnamese. They tease her about her clothes and her accent. Finally, through the clever mediation of the principal, it is Raymond, Ut's former adversary, who becomes her ally and devises a way to reunite her with her mother, who has been unable to come to America. Simple, airy illustrations suggest the cultural hurdles Ut must overcome.

Tran, Khanh-Tuyet
The Little Weaver of Thai-Yen Village
Translated by Christopher Jenkins
Illustrated by Nancy Hom
Children's Book Press, 1987
Ages 8-12, 24 pp.
ISBN 0-89239-030-1

This bilingual book in English and Vietnamese is based on the story of a young Vietnamese girl who was severely injured in a bombing raid during the Vietnam War and brought to America by a humanitarian relief organization for medical treatment. Little Hien survives the bombardment of her village in which her mother and grandmother are killed. She is airlifted to a hospital in the United States for complicated surgery to remove the bomb fragments from her body. When Hien realizes that returning home during the war will not be a simple matter, she decides that there is a contribution she can make to her homeland in a way that is both materially and spiritually fulfilling for her.

Wartski, Maureen Crane
A Boat to Nowhere
Signet Paperbacks, 1981
Ages 12 and up, 152 pp.
ISBN 0-451-16285-4

When their village is overrun by communists, 14-year-old Kien, an orphan, joins other Vietnamese "boat people" on a harrowing flight to freedom across the South China Sea. They survive attack by pirates, gales and sharks, and nearly starve before they are rescued by the crew of an American freighter. In this well-written novel, which is quickly becoming a classic, Kien learns about the bonds that can unite people who undergo adversity together.

The sequel, *A Long Way from Home* (Signet Paperbacks: ISBN 0-451-16035-5), follows Kien as he adjusts to his new life in southern California.

Whelan, Gloria
Goodbye Vietnam
Random House Paperbacks, 1994
Ages 10-16, 136 pp.
ISBN 0-679-82376-X

Refugee camps in present-day Hong Kong are crammed with thousands of Vietnamese refugees who face an uncertain future at best and deportation back to Vietnam at worst, especially if it's decided that they are economic rather than political refugees. In this suspenseful and realistic novel, 13-year-old Mai and her family flee their southern Vietnamese village after they are severely harassed by police. Securing places on a crowded refugee boat, they endure illness, deprivation and despair as they make their way across the sea. Then they face the hardships and frustrations of living in one of Hong Kong's vast refugee camps. Although Mai's family is fortunate enough to be sponsored to the United States, the reader learns that many who have risked so much to reach freedom are not as lucky. An American Library Association Best Book in 1993.

The World Over

Africa

Alexander, Lloyd
The Fortune-Tellers
Illustrated by Trina Schart Hyman
Dutton, 1992
Ages 4-8, unpaged
ISBN 0-525-44849-7

A special treat for readers of all ages, this humorous tale is set in Cameroon but has universal appeal. In it, Lloyd Alexander spins the story of a young African carpenter who goes to an old fortune-teller to try to learn the secrets of his future. When the wizened clairvoyant disappears, the villagers believe he has been transformed into the young, handsome hero who takes a lesson from the seer and becomes known far and wide for his wise prophecies. The flamboyantly detailed illustrations depict the richness of daily village life in Cameroon: a profusion of traditional carvings, jewelry, foods, basketware and brilliantly printed cloths spill over every page. An American Library Association Notable Book in 1993.

Appiah, Sonia
Amoko and Efua Bear
Illustrated by Carol Easmon
Macmillan, 1988
Ages 3-6, unpaged
ISBN 0-02-705591-4

Five-year-old Amoko Efua Mould lives in Ghana. Everywhere she goes, her cherished teddy bear (also named Efua) accompanies her. One day Amoko's Aunt Dinah comes for a visit with a brand-new toy drum for the little girl. In her excitement over the gift, Amoko completely forgets about Efua Bear who is left stranded outside in the dark, a plaything for the dogs. When she realizes next morning that her beloved bear is gone, Amoko is heartbroken—until the two are eventually reunited. While there is nothing particularly innovative about the plot line or prose in this simple book, it effectively enables young children to identify with a familiar experience while catching a glimpse of modern life in Ghana.

Fairman, Tony
Bury My Bones but Keep My Words
Illustrated by Meshack Asare
Henry Holt, 1992
Ages 8 and up, 192 pp.
ISBN 0-8050-233-X

Tales from Kenya, Botswana, Nigeria, Namibia, Gambia and South Africa are exuberantly retold in this collection of 13 traditional and contemporary African stories. The style lends itself particularly to oral storytelling. Tony Fairman is right when he says, "When these tales are told they come alive; they sing, they dance, they laugh, they move, they rattle along." The stories in this anthology fairly jump off the page and cry out to be shared in a storyteller's circle. This book is a wonderful resource for literature and drama classes as well.

Gershator, Phillis
The Iroko-Man: A Yoruba Folktale
Illustrated by Holly C. Kim
Orchard Books, 1994
Ages 4-8, unpaged
ISBN 0-531-06810-2

Reminiscent of the European folktale *Rumpelstiltskin*, *The Iroko-Man* is set in a small Nigerian village where the inhabitants have been long cursed with infertility. In a desperate attempt to bear children, the people appeal to the spirit in the iroko tree, known as the Iroko-Man, whose powerful magic can be used for both good and evil purposes. In exchange for granting them fertility, the Iroko-Man exacts payment from all the villagers. However, the woodcarver's wife, with nothing to give the spirit, in desperation pledges him the life of her promised child. Her husband then outwits the spirit and he and his wife are able to keep their child. Because the ending does not include the demise of the Iroko-Man, it provides a jumping-off point for children to develop more stories based on his deeds.

Grifalconi, Ann
Flyaway Girl
Little, Brown, 1992
Ages 4-8, unpaged
ISBN 0-316-32866-9

Nsia is a young girl who lives in a village high on the banks of the great Niger River. Her mother is expecting another child and the village women are prodding her to make Nsia assume more responsibility at home. Nsia's mother knows that childhood is a fleeting time of joy and discovery, but this year decides that Nsia is old enough to help take part in the preparations for New Year's Day. Nsia is sent to the riverbank to gather the rushes used for weaving the baskets in the Ceremony of Beginnings. Her trip to the river is a flight of the imagination in which she envisions herself carried to the bank on eagle's wings. When she finally arrives at the river, the voices of her ancestors guide her to the realization that it is time to begin growing up and moving forward from childhood. A border drawn from the designs that adorn the villagers' baskets and other decorative items surround the text on each page. *Flyaway Girl* is an excellent complement to other "flight of fancy" books, such as Arthur Dorros' *Abuela* (see page 35) or Faith Ringgold's *Tar Beach* (see page 22).

Also by Ann Grifalconi is the colorful story, *The Village of Round and Square Houses* (Little, Brown, 1986: ISBN 0-316-32862-6). This Caldecott Honor book describes a real village in the remote hills of Cameroon where the men live in square houses while the women dwell in round ones.

Isadora, Rachel
At the Crossroads
Greenwillow Books, 1991
Ages 4-8, unpaged
ISBN 0-688-05270-3 (hardcover)
     0-688-13103-4 (paperback—Mulberry Books)

In a shanty town in the segregated townships of South Africa, it was not unusual to see a crowd of excited children gathered at the bus stop, waiting for their fathers to return from many months away working in the gold mines. These men were gone for long periods and their families were not permitted to join them. Through the eyes of a crowd of children gathered at the crossroads, the joy of the long-awaited reunion is expressed in spare, lyrical prose. An American Library Association Notable Book in 1992.

Kurtz, Jane
Fire on the Mountain
Illustrated by E.B. Lewis
Simon and Schuster, 1994
Ages 6-10, unpaged
ISBN 0-671-88268-6

Growing up in southwestern Ethiopia, author Jane Kurtz heard this simple, timeless story many times. After the untimely death of his parents, Alemayu, a young shepherd boy, journeys to stay with his sister who is the cook for a wealthy man in an Ethiopian village. When the quiet Alemayu becomes involved in a wager with the haughty and boastful merchant, he must spend a night alone on the freezing summit of a mountain with nothing but a thin cloak to protect him from the raging winds and the howling hyenas. When Alemayu survives this ordeal, the rich man discounts his achievement. As a result, Alemayu, his sister and the other household servants decide to teach the cocky master a lesson about the true meaning of courage. Subtle watercolor paintings illustrate this timeless story with a universal message. Though several Amharic words are scattered through the text, they are not always presented in a context that enables readers to understand the cultural concepts involved. Nonetheless, this folktale is well done, and can even be used with secondary school learners.

Leigh, Nila K.
Learning to Swim in Swaziland: A Child's-Eye View of a Southern African Country
Scholastic , 1993
Ages 6-10, unpaged
ISBN 0-590-45938-4

This delightful account of life in Swaziland was written and illustrated by an eight-year-old American girl who lived there for a time with her parents. The illustrations, which vibrantly depict day-to-day life, are complemented by many photographs of Nila's friends, her school and the barren Swazi landscape. Children will learn about the school day in Swaziland, chores around the house, and Nila's encounters with new foods, new family structures and new customs. This book charmingly communicates its message: "You can do all kinds of things you never dreamed you could do. Just like swimming. Just like writing a book. Just like living in Africa."

Margolies, Barbara A.
Rehema's Journey: A Visit in Tanzania
Scholastic, 1990
Ages 5-8, unpaged
ISBN 0-590-42846-2 (hardcover)
    0-590-42847-0 (paperback)

Rehema, a nine-year-old girl who lives in the rural mountains of Tanzania, accompanies her father on a trip to the town of Arusha for the first time. From there, they travel to the Ngorongoro Crater, home of some of the most superb wildlife in Africa. Margolies' color photographs splendidly capture the diversity of the people and the raw beauty of the landscape and wildlife that Rehema and her father encounter along the way. The glossary of Swahili words would serve as a perfect introduction to Muriel and Tom Feelings' terrific Caldecott Award-winning books about the Swahili language and the peoples who speak it: *Jambo Means Hello* (Dial Paperbacks: ISBN 0-8037-4428-5) and *Moja Means One* (Dial Paperbacks: ISBN 0-8037-5711-5).

Mollel, Tololwa M.
The Orphan Boy
Illustrated by Paul Morin
Oxford University Press, 1990
Ages 6 and up, unpaged
ISBN 0-19-540845-4 (paperback)

All his life, an old African man has longed for a child. So he is naturally overjoyed when Kileken, the orphan boy, mysteriously appears. The boy can accomplish a seemingly impossible number of chores in record time and, what's more, during the season of drought he is able to keep the cattle plump and happy. Delighted to have a son at last, the old man is, nevertheless, consumed by curiosity about the secret of the boy's magical abilities. This curiosity brings about his downfall. Winner of the prestigious Governor General's Award for illustration.

Naidoo, Beverley
Journey to Jo'burg: A South African Story
Illustrated by Eric Velasquez
HarperTrophy Paperbacks, 1988
Ages 9-12, 80 pp.
ISBN 0-06-440237-1

When their baby sister becomes dangerously ill, there is no money for hospital care or for the medicine that might save little Dineo's life. So 13-year-old Naledi and her younger brother, Tiro, decide to slip away on a journey of more than 300 kilometers to Johannesburg, where their mother works as a domestic for a white family. Traveling without passes, the two make their way by foot and truck to the city, where they are flabbergasted to see the luxury in which the suburban white city dwellers live. The children stay with a friend in Soweto, who introduces them to the painful struggle for freedom and dignity that is taking place around them. A moving book about a journey of realization, this book can be used effectively as a novel study with older English as a second language learners.

Chain of Fire (HarperTrophy Paperbacks, 1993: ISBN 0-06-440468-4) is the equally powerful sequel to this book. In it, Naledi and her brother join in a student demonstration after the inhabitants of their village are forced to resettle in a barren "homeland."

Williams, Karen Lynn
Galimoto
Illustrated by Catherine Stock
Lothrop, Lee & Shepard, 1990
Ages 4-8, unpaged
ISBN 0-688-08789-2 (hardcover)
0-688-10991-8 (paperback—Mulberry Books)

Kondi, a young boy in Malawi, wants to make a *galimoto*, a kind of push toy many children in his village fashion from sticks, stalks or wires. But Kondi doesn't have enough wire and, besides, nobody believes a seven-year-old can actually build a *galimoto*. The determined boy employs all his wiles to amass enough of the precious wire to construct his own plaything and, by day's end, happily joins the procession of children wheeling their toys along the village paths. A note informs readers that the word *galimoto* originates in the English "motor car." Featured on the PBS series *Reading Rainbow*, this timeless story of a young child who steadfastly takes matters into his own hands to make his small dream come true will strike a chord with preschool and young primary children.

Illustrator Catherine Stock's picture book, *Where Are You Going, Manyoni?* (Morrow, 1993: ISBN 0-688-10352-9), presents an equally successful portrayal of the daily life of a young African girl, this time in the veld of Zimbabwe.

Wisniewski, David
Sundiata, Lion King of Mali
Clarion Books, 1992
Ages 6-10, unpaged
ISBN 0-395-61302-7

Marvelously intricate papercuts illustrate this story about the triumph of Sundiata, exiled prince of Mali, over the ruler of the neighboring kingdom of Sosso. A great battle took place between their forces more than 700 years ago after Sundiata, a weak and sickly prince, was driven from his homeland, only to return as a courageous leader and drive out the invading enemy. Drawing on stories passed down by African *griots* (oral historians), author-illustrator David Wisniewski has gone to great lengths to ensure historical accuracy, both in the text and the visual depiction of Sundiata's life. The resulting volume is a treat for the eye, and an excellent choice for a picture book or storytelling unit for adolescent or adult learners. An American Library Association Notable Book in 1993.

Canada

Andrews, Jan
Very Last First Time
Illustrated by Ian Wallace
Groundwood Books, 1985
Ages 4-8, unpaged
ISBN 0-88899-043-X

Eva Padlyat is an Inuit girl living in a village on Ungava Bay in northern Quebec. When the tide is out in winter, the people of her village chisel a hole in the thick layer of ice covering the bay and descend to the seabed to collect mussels. One day, Eva's mother decides that Eva is ready to make the trip down to the seabed by herself. A warm and sensitive portrayal of a child's pride in achieving something new and grown-up, this book also presents a genuinely balanced view of contemporary Inuit life. Eva wears a parka and mukluks and uses snowshoes, but she also lives in a modern home, eats corn flakes and fastens her artwork up on the fridge with magnets. Ian Wallace's illustrations convincingly convey both the cold of the climate and the warmth of the people.

Bannatyne-Cugnet, Jo & Yvette Moore
A Prairie Alphabet
Tundra Books, 1992
Ages 4-8, unpaged
ISBN 0-88776-292-1

"We wade through the wheat waving in the wind." So reads the entry for W, in this captivating alphabet book, which paints an alliterative portrait of life on the Canadian Prairies. Each finely executed illustration is also a puzzle in which children can search for a variety of items beginning with the same letter. Notes at the back of the book provide additional background on the Prairies for those who don't know the difference between canola and millet.

Bouchard, David
If You're Not from the Prairie...
Illustrated by Henry Ripplinger
Raincoast Books, 1993
Ages 6 and up, unpaged
ISBN 0-9696097-4-4

The Prairie landscape occupies a special place in the hearts and minds of Canadians born and raised there. In this stunning book, two Saskatchewan natives take readers on a visual and poetic journey to the plains of their childhood. The cutting of the fierce winter wind, the whisper of the tall grass, and the high, blinding snowdrifts are all beautifully evoked in author David Bouchard's lyrical poem. Henry Ripplinger's illustrations, so real and finely detailed that they almost appear to be photographs, provide a beautiful complement to the bittersweet text, which celebrates the joys and remembers the hardships of life on the Canadian Prairie.

Carrier, Roch
The Hockey Sweater
Illustrated by Sheldon Cohen
Tundra Books, 1979
Ages 5-10, unpaged
ISBN 0-88776-169 (hardcover)
        0-88776-174-7 (paperback)

Any fan who has ever rooted for the hometown team will enjoy this Canadian classic about a rural Quebec boy who worships that greatest hockey idol of all time, Maurice—the Rocket—Richard of the mighty Montreal Canadiens, and whose passion is to spend every free moment playing hockey. When the boy's new hockey sweater arrives by mail order from the city, though, he is horrified to find that the department store has made a ghastly mistake and sent him a Toronto Maple Leafs sweater! What happens when the boy is forced to wear the dreaded sweater is the stuff of belly laughs. Sheldon Cohen's colorful and childlike drawings perfectly evoke the feel of postwar rural Quebec, when the careers of the great stars of hockey were at their zenith.

Doyle, Brian
Spud Sweetgrass
Groundwood Books, 1992
Ages 10-14, 140 pp.
ISBN 0-88899-189-4

Set in Ottawa, *Spud Sweetgrass* humorously confronts many contemporary concerns, such as racism, multiculturalism and environmental issues. John—"Call me 'Spud'"—Sweetgrass has been thrown out of Ottawa Tech for rudeness to a teacher and has set up his own chip wagon in Ottawa's Chinatown. Then he discovers that someone is dumping grease into the Ottawa River, ruining the beach where he and his girlfriend play volleyball with the kids from the school's ESL program. Watching Spud learn about life as he tries to solve the problems of the world and cook the perfect french fry is an entertaining adventure.

Harrison, Ted
O Canada!
Kids Can Press, 1992
Ages 6 and up, unpaged
ISBN 1-55074-087-3

The complete text—in both French and English—of Canada's national anthem, including two verses that are all but unknown to most Canadians, unrolls across the pages of this book to the accompaniment of artist Ted Harrison's strikingly colored artistic impressions of each Canadian province and territory. This illustrated edition of "O Canada" includes background notes on the song's origins, as well as Harrison's own brief descriptions of the beauty and unique character of each province. A stunning introduction to Canada for children.

McFarlane, Sheryl
Waiting for the Whales
Illustrated by Ron Lightburn
Orca Book Publishers, 1991
Ages 5-10, unpaged
ISBN 0-920501-66-4

In this timeless story set on the Pacific coast, a lonely old man lives by himself on a bluff overlooking the sea. His loneliness eases only when the whales return each year to the bay in front of his cottage. One day, his daughter and her baby return home to live with him, bringing a renewed sense of purpose to his life. As his granddaughter grows, the elderly man passes on to her his knowledge and insight, as well as his passion for whales. Every year, they wait together for the whales to appear. A gentle story that illuminates the friendship between grandparent and child, *Waiting for the Whales* also suggests that aging and death are part of a greater cycle of rebirth and continuity. Winner of many honors, including the Governor General's Award.

McGugan, Jim
Josepha: A Prairie Boy's Story
Illustrated by Murray Kimber
Red Deer College Press, 1994
Ages 6-10, 32 pp.
ISBN 0-88995-101-2

It is 1900. A young Prairie boy must say goodbye to his older schoolmate, Josepha, an immigrant who is leaving behind the alien world of the classroom where no one speaks his language. Although Josepha's school year has been marked by poverty and hardship, his young Canadian companion has helped him discover the true meaning of friendship. This poetically written story offers insight into the immigrant's struggle to begin again in a strange land and will strike a familiar chord with contemporary immigrant children. The illustrations, in piercing hues of blue, green and brown, evoke the stark reality of Josepha's difficult life. Winner of the 1994 Governor General's Award for illustration.

Morgan, Allen
The Magic Hockey Skates
Illustrated by Michael Martchenko
Oxford University Press, 1991
Ages 4-8, unpaged
ISBN 0-19-540823-3 (hardcover)
    0-19-540851-9 (paperback)

When hockey season arrives, Joey finds that, once again, his old skates are too small. At the department store, he is disappointed when his dad insists on buying him a secondhand pair. But the clerk at the checkout counter whispers that these skates are special: Joey can make three wishes about skating come true by rubbing the toes while making a wish. Skeptical, Joey nevertheless tries out the skates—and the wishes—and finds that his skating has greatly improved by the end of the morning hockey practice. The skates really might be magic! This is a lovely story of a young boy who gains self-confidence through the "magic" of believing in his enchanted skates and in himself.

Poulin, Stéphane
Ah! Belle cité! A Beautiful City
Tundra Books, 1985
Ages 3-8, unpaged
ISBN 0-88776-175-5

This imaginatively bilingual alphabet book is an excellent vehicle for acquainting young children with the concept of Canada's two national languages. Each letter of the alphabet is matched with both a French and an English word, usually derivatives of the same Latin root. There are some witty diversions from the usual alphabetical associations; for example, N for navel and *nombril* and A for antique dealer and *antiquaire*. But even Stéphane Poulin's wit cannot help him escape from the inevitable "xylophone." The illustrations for each letter take readers on a visual tour of picturesque and unusual corners of Montreal, Poulin's hometown and Canada's premier bilingual city. Author's notes in both languages explain the significance of each Montreal scene. As an added diversion and reinforcement of the alphabet concept, each painting contains pictures of three other things that also begin with the same letter in both French and English.

Service, Robert W.
The Cremation of Sam McGee
Illustrated by Ted Harrison
Kids Can Press, 1987
All ages, 32 pp.
ISBN 0-919964-92-3

As a young bank clerk posted to Whitehorse and Dawson City in the Canadian Yukon in the early 20th century, poet Robert Service had ample opportunity to witness the rugged lives of the trappers, miners and hunters who came to seek their fortunes in the North.

This classic Service poem is about a subject familiar to every Northerner—the fierce cold and what it can do to a man, physically and spiritually. Service's fiercely rhythmical poem combines awe of nature, sadness and humor, elements that are mirrored in Ted Harrison's paintings, which add some whimsical flourishes to the more outrageous events in the poem's narrative. Harrison has also illustrated another Service masterpiece, *The Shooting of Dan McGrew* (Kids Can Press, 1988: ISBN 0-921103-35-2), a wild-west-style story of betrayal and revenge in a Klondike gold rush saloon.

Tundra Books
Canadian Childhoods
Tundra Books, 1989
Ages 8 and up, 96 pp.
ISBN 0-88776-208-5

Tundra Books, publisher of outstanding Canadian children's literature, celebrated its 20th anniversary by releasing this beautiful collection of excerpts from a variety of books published during its first two decades. From Sing Lim's "A Chinese Boyhood on the West Coast," to Carlo Italiano's "Montreal: A City of Sleighs," to Frederick Ward's "On Being Black in Nova Scotia," the 17 excerpts present the experiences of children of many backgrounds growing up across Canada. The anthology is beautifully illustrated with artwork from each of the original books, including William Kurelek's expansive prairie landscapes and Gordon Roache's depictions of stormy Halifax harbor. This book is a treat for both the eyes and the mind.

Caribbean

Agard, John
The Calypso Alphabet
Illustrated by Jennifer Bent
Henry Holt, 1989
Ages 4-8, unpaged
ISBN 0-8050-1177-3

This wonderful alphabet book pulses with the cadences of Caribbean English. From *Anancy* to *zombie* with *jook* and *kaiso* in between, 26 words and phrases indigenous to the Caribbean islands are accompanied by poetry and lush illustrations that introduce young readers to the sights and sounds of the region. A word list explains all the unfamiliar terms. This book is excellent for encouraging older learners to compile their own alphabet lists and poems reflecting the atmosphere and style of their own native regions or countries.

Agard, John & Grace Nichols, Eds.
A Caribbean Dozen: Poems from Caribbean Poets
Illustrated by Cathie Felstead
Candlewick Press, 1994
Ages 6-12, 93 pp.
ISBN 1-56402-339-7

In the bustling markets of the Caribbean islands, the vendors have a tradition of throwing in an extra handful of fish or fruit in a generous gesture of *mek-up*. In keeping with this congenial custom, *A Caribbean Dozen* presents a collection of works by 13 writers who convey the experiences of their island childhoods through poetry and prose. Accompanied by Cathie Felstead's artwork in a variety of styles united by their colorful representation of island life, this book is a wonderful introduction to well-known poets such as John Agard and James Berry, as well as to lesser-known authors like Jamaican-born Opal Palmer Adisa and Guyanese Canadian David Campbell.

Berry, James
Ajeemah and His Son
HarperCollins, 1992
Ages 12 and up, 83 pp.
ISBN 0-06-021044-3

It's 1807, one year before the enactment of a British law that will stop the African slave trade. As a result, the kidnapping of Africans has intensified as slave traders anticipate that their lucrative source of income will soon disappear. On the eve of his marriage to Sisi, Atu and his father, Ajeemah, are journeying to Sisi's village to deliver a dowry of gold to the family of his bride-to-be. Suddenly, they are ambushed by slave traders, blindfolded, bound and herded onto a huge clanking ship full of imprisoned Africans. Taken to Jamaica, the father and son are cruelly separated and sold to different plantation owners, never to see each other again.

This beautifully written saga draws us into the world of slavery as seen through the eyes of the human chattels of this diabolical economic system. As we watch the dashing of one man's hopes and the gradual acceptance of his fate by the other, we appreciate the very individual reactions of two men caught in a morass of misery and exploitation. Winner of the Boston Globe/Horn Book Award for children's literature, *Ajeemah and His Son* is also included in James Berry's 1991 collection of seven Caribbean stories, *The Future-Telling Lady* (Puffin Books, 1991: ISBN 0-14-034763-1).

Bryan, Ashley
Turtle Knows Your Name
Atheneum Books, 1989
Ages 3-8, unpaged
ISBN 0-689-31578 (hardcover)
  0-689-71728-8 (paperback—Aladdin Paperbacks)

A small Caribbean boy has a very, very long name: Upsilmana Tumpalerado. His granny patiently teaches it to him over and over until one day he is grown enough to master this mouthful of a moniker. Though she commiserates with the boy on his lengthy name, she often mysteriously hints, "Your name is long, but it's not the longest." In this lively retelling of a West Indian tale, Upsilimana Tumpalerado comes to solve Granny's puzzling riddle with the help of a magical turtle at the water's edge. Young children will enjoy chanting along with the repetitive and rhythmical names of the characters.

Another book with a similarly pleasing Caribbean gibberish refrain is Phillis Gershator's *Rata-pata-scata-fata* (Little, Brown, 1994: ISBN 0-316-30470-0), in which an old-time Virgin Islands' nonsense phrase magically helps a young boy do his dreaded household chores.

Bryan, Ashley
The Dancing Granny
Aladdin Paperbacks, 1987
Ages 5-10, 64 pp.
ISBN 0-689-71149-2

Granny Anika produces a lush variety of okra, corn, beets and yams in her vegetable garden. But what she likes to do best while she is tilling and weeding is dance and spin to the beat of her hoe and the rhythms of her own songs. In fact, she can get so caught up in her dancing that she does cartwheels through the furrows. In this Anansi tale, the ubiquitous trickster plots to get Granny dancing so he can raid her garden. But of course, in the end, Spider Anansi is taken in by his own trick as Dancing Granny Anika turns the tables on him. An audiocassette version of this lively Caribbean story, read by the author who is a talented storyteller, is also available (Caedmon Audiocassette; ISBN 1-55994-046-8).

Carlstrom, Nancy White
Baby-O
Illustrated by Sucie Stevenson
Little, Brown, 1992
Ages 3-6, unpaged
ISBN 0-316-12851-1

In this lively cumulative tale, three generations of a West Indian family gather on a jitney that takes them and their wares to the local market. Children will love to chant, clap and stamp along with the rhythmic text and nonsense sounds that describe what happens as each member of the extended family loads a different item—mangoes, fish, baskets, vegetables and cloth—aboard the jitney and it chugs happily over the green mountainside to town.

Gershator, Phillis
Tukama Tootles the Flute: A Tale from the Antilles
Orchard Books, 1994
Ages 4-8, unpaged
ISBN 0-531-06811-0

Tukama is quite the wild thing. Instead of helping his grandmother fetch water or dig potatoes, he's off clambering up and down the dangerous rocky cliffs by the sea, all the while tootling on his flute. Of course, the lazy Tukama manages to get himself into a big pile of mischief, in this tale from St. Thomas, which is reminiscent of *Jack and the Beanstalk*. Bold color-block illustrations accompany the text, which is spiced with the wonderful West Indian incantations that Tukama uses to extricate himself from his predicaments.

Gonzalez, Lucia M.
The Bossy Gallito/El Gallo de Bodas
Illustrated by Lulu Delacre
Scholastic, 1994
Ages 3-8, unpaged
ISBN 0-590-46843-X

A cumulative tale reminiscent of *Chicken Little*, *The Bossy Gallito* is the story of a very pushy rooster who is all dressed up for the wedding of his uncle, Tio Perico. On the way to the wedding, he greedily scoops up some corn kernels from a mud puddle, dirties his beak, and commands an entire cast of unwilling characters to clean it for him. With the help of his friend *el sol*, the sun, he finally exacts some compliance and arrives at the wedding ceremony in time. The cheerful text in both English and Spanish and the repetitive pattern of this story are especially suited to learners of English or Spanish as a second language. The text is enhanced by a glossary, as well as by three pages of fascinating short notes about Cuban folklore and Hispanic Caribbean customs. Lucia Gonzalez originally hails from Havana, and remembers this tale as an integral part of her Cuban childhood.

Gunning, Monica
Not a Copper Penny in Me House
Illustrated by Frané Lessac
Boyds Mills Press, 1993
Ages 6-12, 32 pp.
ISBN 1-56397-050-3

Jamaican-born teacher and author Monica Gunning has written a complete set of original poems for her new book *Not a Copper Penny in Me House*. This collection portrays one child's life in the Caribbean—picking sorrel, making a Christmas red wine, peeping out through the shutters in the darkness of a tropical hurricane, listening to the competitive shouts of banana hawkers at the roadside and watching the clean white laundry of the entire village bleaching in the sun on Monday morning. The artwork by the superb island artist Frané Lessac completes this delightful book.

Hodge, Merle
For the Life of Laetitia
Farrar, Straus & Giroux, 1993
Ages 10-14, 214 pp.
ISBN 0-374-32447-6 (hardcover)
      0-374-42444-6 (paperback)

Laetitia Johnson, Lacey for short, has just been accepted at the government secondary school in the faraway town of La Puerta. There is much rejoicing about her achievement, but it comes at a price: the only way Lacey can afford to attend the school is if she moves away from her grandparents' village home and goes to live in La Puerta with her father, who is a virtual stranger to her, and his new wife and child. As the semester progresses, Lacey realizes that achieving success in her new life depends on more than good grades at school. Under pressure from her father and some of her teachers to look down on her rural roots, Lacey struggles to keep her pride intact. But it isn't until tragedy strikes her new-found best friend Anjanee that Lacey is forced to see beyond herself and her homesickness and come to terms with both her worlds. This realistic portrayal of a child's life in the Caribbean was named an American Library Association Notable Book in 1994.

Joseph, Lynn
Coconut Kind of Day: Island Poems
Illustrated by Sandra Speidel
Lothrop, Lee & Shepard, 1990
Ages 4-10, unpaged
ISBN 0-688-09119-9

More anchored in island dialect than Monica Gunning's *Not a Copper Penny in Me House* (see page 74), the poems of Trinidad native Lynn Joseph also resonate with the soul of a child's experiences growing up in the Caribbean. The rhythmic word play and cadences of the sound poems are especially appealing to younger children.

Joseph, Lynn
A Wave in Her Pocket: Stories from Trinidad
Illustrated by Brian Pinkney
Clarion Books, 1991
Ages 8-12, 52 pp.
ISBN 0-395-54432-7

Practically every family in Trinidad has a *tantie*, a wise and experienced grandaunt who helps take care of her grandnieces and nephews and keeps them spellbound with stories that make them laugh, shiver and reflect on their connections to their people. In this collection, Amber and her cousins settle down on six different occasions while their *tantie* tells traditional stories about graveyard *jumbies* (bogeymen) and a village woman who could peel off her skin and turn herself into a *soucouyant*, a blood-sucking, whirling ball of fire. Told in the distinctive cadences of the Trinidad dialect, this is an appealing and colorful collection of West Indian folklore.

Keens-Douglas, Richardo
La Diablesse and the Baby
Illustrated by Marie Lafrance
Annick Press, 1994
Ages 5-10, unpaged
ISBN 1-55037-992-5

This is a wonderfully eerie retelling of a story about *la diablesse*, the mythical Caribbean phantom who can steal your soul and tries to snatch other people's babies out of jealousy because she has no children of her own.

On a stormy night, a young stranger approaches Grandmother's door as she is lulling the baby to sleep. The stranger ingratiates her way into the house, but Grandmother, becoming suspicious that the visitor is, in fact, *la diablesse*, is on guard against all her ruses. Spooky, dark illustrations add atmosphere to this tale, told so compellingly that we can almost hear the whisper of the storyteller's voice as the suspense builds to a climax.

Also by Richardo Keens-Douglas is *The Nutmeg Princess* (Annick Press, 1992: ISBN 1-55037-239-4—hardcover; 1-55037-236-X—paperback), a magical tale of how nutmeg came to be the most precious crop of Granada, the Caribbean "Isle of Spice." The illustrations are beautifully impressionistic and filled with a rainbow of lush, hot colors evocative of the setting.

Keller, Holly
Island Baby
Greenwillow Books, 1992
Ages 4-8, unpaged
ISBN 0-688-10579-3

On a small Caribbean island lives Pops, a grandfatherly white-haired fellow who runs a hospital for sick and injured wild birds. Simon, Pops' young assistant, helps him rescue a flamingo with a broken leg who has crashed on the sea rocks, then joins Pops in nursing the bird back to health. Inevitably, Simon learns an important lesson about freedom and independence, which Keller relates to Simon's own life in an understated way that children can easily understand.

Lessac, Frané, Ed.
Caribbean Canvas
J.B. Lippincott, 1987
All ages, unpaged
ISBN 0-397-32367-0

The artwork of Caribbean-born illustrator Frané Lessac accompanies this brief collection of poems and proverbs by various West Indian poets. Selections such as "Kinky Hair Blues" and "The Song of the Banana Man," mostly in island dialect, combine with Lessac's illustrations of life on Montserrat, Barbados, Antigua and St. Kitts to create an evocative picture book with appeal for all ages.

Lessac, Frané
The Little Island
Macmillan Caribbean, 1984
Ages 3-8, unpaged
ISBN 0-333-38009-6

Frané Lessac's colorful paintings of island life buzz with an energy that complements the simple text of this book. Watching the fisherman haul in their catch, shopping for fresh nutmeg and juicy orange pawpaws in the busy market, dropping by the school for a visit with old friends or dancing in a jump-up at carnival, the young narrator takes us on a lively tour of a small Caribbean island.

Linden, Ann Marie
One Smiling Grandma: A Caribbean Counting Book
Dial Books for Young Readers, 1992
Ages 3-6, unpaged
ISBN 0-8037-1132-8

A little Caribbean girl anticipates spending her holiday with her grandmother, when they will see many exciting things around their island home. Based on Ann Marie Linden's memories of her own West Indian childhood, this simple yet evocative counting rhyme is accompanied by vibrant illustrations of scenes from the island, such as sugar apple trees, conch shells on the shore, hummingbirds gathering nectar, and the pulsing of a steel drum band.

Mitchell, Rita Phillips
Hue Boy
Illustrated by Caroline Binch
Victor Gollancz, 1992
Ages 4-8, unpaged
ISBN 0-575-04798-4

Little Hue Boy has a big problem. He is short, so small that all his friends at school tower over him. As a result, everyone in the village has a suggestion for increasing his height. From bowls of Mum's pumpkin soup, to his neighbor's stretching exercises, to the village healer's incantations and herbal baths, Hue Boy will try anything to add a few centimeters to his tiny frame. But, despite his diligent efforts, nothing seems to work and Hue Boy remains the shortest boy in school as well as the object of a lot of teasing about high-heeled shoes—until one day his father returns from a very long stint at sea and, walking beside him, Hue Boy holds his head taller than ever before. The warm simplicity of the text and the beautiful color-washed illustrations evoke touching images of life in a Caribbean village.

Orr, Katherine
My Grandpa and the Sea
Carolrhoda Books, 1990
Ages 5-9, unpaged
ISBN 0-87614-409-1 (hardcover)
 0-87614-525-X (paperback)

A traditional fisherman on the island of St. Lucia, Lil's grandfather can no longer compete with the sophisticated new trawlers that younger fisherman are acquiring. But the sea has been his whole life and, now that it no longer offers him the opportunity to make his living, he is at loose ends. Grandpa is scornful of the new high-tech fishermen who, he says, "...come to God's table with a wheelbarrow instead of a plate. You cannot prosper by taking more than God can give." A chance remark at dinner one night gives Grandpa an idea that will enable him to renew his connection with the sea, make a living, and continue to give something back for everything he takes from the sea. The environmental theme, so timely now in view of the overfishing crisis in Atlantic Canada, is complemented by the bright and beautiful illustrations that convey the beauty and balance of nature in the Caribbean.

Philip, Marlene Nourbese
Harriet's Daughter
The Women's Press, 1988
Ages 12-16, 150 pp.
ISBN 0-88961-134-3 (paperback)

Narrated by Margaret Cruickshank, a bright and irrepressible 14-year-old, this is the story of two adolescent friends in Toronto's West Indian community who slowly develop the courage to walk a different path from their mothers. Observing how her mother is dominated by her strict disciplinarian father, Margaret idolizes her heroine, the Underground Railroad conductor Harriet Tubman, and directs this positive energy into achieving her teenage goal of a more independent life. Her best friend Zulma must live in a home where her stepfather physically abuses her mother, and dreams of somehow putting together the plane fare that will enable her to return to live with her grandmother in Tobago. Apart from the strong feminist theme of women's empowerment that runs through the story, issues of ethnicity and adolescent identity are dealt with in a humorous and insightful way in this fine young adult novel.

Temple, Frances
Taste of Salt
HarperTrophy, 1994
Ages 12-16, 179 pp.
ISBN 0-06-447136-5 (paperback)

The victim of a terrible fire-bombing, 17-year-old Djo lies in agony in his hospital bed in Port-au-Prince, Haiti. A member of Father Jean-Bertrand Aristide's fighters against Haiti's military dictatorship, Djo summons the energy and courage to tell the story of his involvement in the resistance to Jeremie, another Haitian teenager who has come to his bedside with a tape recorder at Aristide's request. Jeremie has her own story of oppression, too, and the two young people's voices interweave in this powerful novel of the hard choices facing Haiti's youth.

Williams, Karen Lynn
Tap-Tap
Illustrated by Catherine Stock
Clarion Books, 1994
Ages 5-9, 34 pp.
ISBN 0-395-65617-6

Eight-year-old Sasifi and her mother carry their straw baskets of oranges on their heads as they walk along the road toward the village market. After selling all their produce in the bustling marketplace, the Haitian girl and her mother have enough money left to ride home in a tap-tap, one of the brightly painted trucks that pick up passengers and let them off when they bang out a signal on the side of the vehicle. This satisfying story of Haitian village life paints a realistic portrait of the daily joys and adventures of a young island girl.

Wolkstein, Diane
The Magic Orange Tree and Other Haitian Folktales
Illustrated by Elsa Henriquez
Schocken Books, 1978
Ages 10 and up, 212 pp.
ISBN 0-8052-0650-7

In the 1970s, Diane Wolkstein traveled to Haiti, where she visited innumerable village storytellers. This collection of authentic Haitian tales is transcribed from the copious notes and recordings she made during her visit. Though many of the tales have a sub-text of hunger and poverty, which is always present in the lives of Haitian peasants, they also display humor, imagination and insight. As audience participation is *de rigueur* in Haitian storytelling, many of the stories also contain *contes chantes*, songs that are chanted by everyone present at a storytelling session.

Central and South America

Ancona, George
The Piñata Maker/El Piñatero
Harcourt Brace, 1994
Ages 6-12, unpaged
ISBN 0-15-200060-7

Don Ricardo, or Tio Rico, as the children have nicknamed him, is the *piñata* maker in the village of Ejutla de Crespo in southern Mexico. Formerly a maker of felt *sombreros*, Don Ricardo channeled his creative energies into *piñata*-making when it became too difficult for him to work at the hot fire needed for shaping the *sombreros*. Now 77 years old, he has been fashioning intricate and colorful *piñatas*, puppets and masks for the village *fiestas*, pageants, birthday parties and celebrations for the past 15 years. Told in both English and Spanish and highlighted by full-color photographs, *The Piñata Maker* painstakingly documents this traditional art form, as a stack of old newspapers is transformed into an intricately styled swan and an elaborate many-pointed star.

Blanco, Alberta
Angel's Kite
Illustrated by Rodolfo Morales
Children's Book Press, 1994
Ages 4-8, 32 pp.
ISBN 0-89239-121-9

In a small Mexican town that would be perfect were it not for the missing bell in the church on the town square, a young boy named Angel sells kites. Angel takes great pleasure in crafting the colorful handmade kites that bring his imagination to life. One day, one of Angel's kites escapes on the wind and, by the end of the adventure, the long-missing church bell has mysteriously returned and is once again pealing over the *fiesta* in the plaza. Bright collage pictures of paper, string, buttons and lace accompany the text, written in both Spanish and English.

Cameron, Ann
The Most Beautiful Place in the World
Knopf/Bullseye Paperbacks, 1993
Ages 6-12, 57 pp.
ISBN 0-394-80424-4

San Pablo, a town in the Guatemala mountains, is on the edge of a shining lake surrounded by rippling hills covered in cornfields and coffee trees. The flower-filled town is alive with the songs of wild parrots and hummingbirds. But for young Juan, life is less than beautiful. His mother has abandoned him to his grandmother, who rises at 5 a.m. every day to prepare the *arroz con leche*, a sort of rice pudding, that she sells in the market square. Juan, too, must shine shoes all day to contribute to the family's survival. But his dream is to stop working and attend school, and his challenge is to make his grandmother realize just how important this is to him.

Castañeda, Omar S.
Abuela's Weave
Illustrated by Enrique O. Sanchez
Lee and Low Books, 1993
Ages 4-9, 32 pp.
ISBN 1-880000-00-8

In their Guatemalan village of Santa Cruz, Esperanza's *abuela* (grandmother) is unequalled in her talent for weaving traditional and colorful Mayan tapestries, and she is passing on all she knows to her young granddaughter. Side by side, the old woman and Esperanza sit at their hand looms, producing a new cloth of special brilliance and intricacy that they plan to sell at the city market. However, to avoid scaring customers away, they must deal realistically with the townsfolk's superstitions about the splotchy red birthmark on Abuela's cheek. As a result, Esperanza must navigate the city streets and negotiate with buyers on her own, as Abuela shadows her nearby, her head draped in a thick shawl. This authentic and sensitive portrayal of life in the developing world was a Parents' Choice Foundation Honor book in 1993. A special artistic touch is the woven tapestry design on the hardcover, which peeps out temptingly from beneath the book's paper jacket.

Castañeda, Omar S.
Among the Volcanoes
Dell Paperbacks, 1991
Ages 10-14, 183 pp.
ISBN 0-440-40746-X

Isabel Pacay, a young woman living with her struggling family in rural Guatemala, is expected to marry her handsome suitor; but she has a conflicting goal—to become a teacher. The theme—finding a middle ground between traditional and modern life—is developed in a number of ways. For example, Isabel's ill mother refuses Western medical treatment, preferring to place her faith in the village healer. This novel effectively presents the complex issues involved in giving aid to developing countries and the resistance of local peoples to technological change, which doesn't always represent true progress.

In the sequel, *Imagining Isabel* (Lodestar Books, 1994: ISBN 0-525-67431-4), newly married Isabel enrols in a teacher-training program in a faraway town where she experiences a political awakening.

Dorros, Arthur
Tonight Is Carnaval
Illustrated with *arpilleras* sewn by the Club de Madres Virgen del Carmen of Lima, Peru
Dutton, 1991
Ages 5-8, unpaged
ISBN 0-525-44641-9 (hardcover)
  0-14-055467-X (paperback—Puffin Unciorn)

A joint venture of Oxfam America and Dutton Children's Books, *Tonight Is Carnaval* reveals the daily life of a young Peruvian boy as he and his family finish all the work in the fields in anticipation of the forthcoming carnival. The life of rural farmers in the high Andes Mountains as they shear alpaca wool, dig potatoes and sell their crops at the village market is depicted. The story is accompanied by a series of specially commissioned *arpilleras*, which are traditional wall-hangings put together from scraps of brightly colored cloth. A short photo essay captures the Peruvian women in the process of sewing the vibrant story cloths, and there is a glossary of typical South American folk instruments. The endpapers of the book are a brilliant visual dictionary in Spanish of Andean vegetables crafted on another imaginative *arpillera*.

Ehlert, Lois
Moon Rope: A Peruvian Folktale
Harcourt, Brace, 1992
Ages 4-8, unpaged
ISBN 0-15-255343-6

In this adaption of a Peruvian *pourquoi* tale that tells us why the mole burrows underground, the fox and the mole collaborate to try to climb to the moon on a woven grass rope. Lois Ehlert uses an ancient South American motif in her illustrations, many of which are done in shimmering silver reminiscent of the moon's glow. The text is in both English and Spanish, with the Spanish paragraphs in a silvery metallic font. This beautifully simple story will delight young children.

Johnston, Tony
The Old Lady and the Birds
Illustrated by Stephanie Garcia
Harcourt Brace, 1994
Ages 3-8, unpaged
ISBN 0-15-257769-6

The intricate artwork that graces this simple story about an old lady who sits under the pepper tree in her verdant Mexican garden will enthrall children and adults alike. As the sun moves across the brilliant blue sky, the spare story follows the old woman through a day—breakfasting on fresh *bolillos*, lunching on *tortillas*, and napping with the sleek cat curled happily on her lap. The dazzling illustrations—in reality three-dimensional models of the garden, lush with flowers, birds and colorful pottery—are constructed of a variety of materials including clay, foil, wire, cloth, wood and feathers—may inspire older readers to try their hand at building their own models.

Markun, Patricia Maloney
The Little Painter of Sabana Grande
Illustrated by Robert Casilla
Bradbury Press, 1993
Ages 4-8, unpaged
ISBN 0-02-762205-3

In the village of Sabana Grande, high in the mountains of Panama, Fernando Espino is just starting his dry-season vacation from school. Having just learned to draw colored pictures with crayons, Fernando is determined to learn to paint during his vacation, and carefully collects all the berries, charcoal and clay he needs to make his own paints. But the lack of a surface on which to paint poses a problem, until he thinks of an idea that transforms his school vacation—and the entire village of Sabana Grande.

Orozco, José-Luis
De Colores and Other Latin-American Folk Songs for Children
Illustrated by Elisa Kleven
Dutton Children's Books, 1994
Ages 5-12, 56 pp.
ISBN 0-525-45260-5

Twenty-seven songs, chants and rhymes from South America are collected in this colorful volume. Explanatory notes, simple musical arrangements for piano and guitar, and the original Spanish lyrics and their English translations are surrounded on each page by Elisa Kleven's fantastical illustrated borders. The traditional holiday songs, lullabies, nursery rhymes and even a Spanish version of "The Eensy, Weensy Spider" will encourage children to enjoy and share Latin-American music.

Pomerantz, Charlotte
The Tamarindo Puppy and Other Poems
Illustrated by Byron Barton
Mulberry Books, 1993
Ages 3-7, 32 pp.
ISBN 0-688-11514-4 (paperback)

The 13 poems in this illustrated collection flow effortlessly back and forth between Spanish and English in a joyful salute to a bilingual childhood. Verses like "...thirty small kisses, Maria. *Treinta besitos*, one for each day," and "*Mariposa*, butterfly, *Mariposa*, fluttering by," give children who don't speak Spanish plenty of opportunity to grasp the meaning of words in a new language. The only poem actually presented in a complete translation is "You—*Tu*," a short rhyme about peeking in the mirror, in which the English and Spanish texts along with the illustrations are cleverly presented in a sort of visual mirror metaphor.

Arroz con Leche: Popular Songs and Rhymes from Latin America (Scholastic, 1989: ISBN 0-590-41887-4) is another bilingual anthology of songs and rhymes for the same age group. In this collection, Lulu Delacre has selected and illustrated traditional nursery ditties and melodies from Mexico, Puerto Rico and Argentina.

Winter, Jeanette
Diego
Text by Jonah Winter
Knopf, 1991
Ages 4-10, unpaged
ISBN 0-679-81987-8

Winner of the *New York Times* Award for best-illustrated children's book, *Diego* tells the story of Mexican muralist Diego Rivera. Rivera's special accomplishment was to bring art out of the corridors of museums and splash it onto the walls of public buildings so that everyone would have access to it. With kaleidoscopic miniature paintings of the influential moments in Rivera's life, artist Jeanette Winter conveys both his love for art and for Mexico. The spare, straightforward text appears in both English and Spanish. Among the interesting notes contained in the afterword is the information that the prolific Rivera painted more than 2½ linear miles of murals during his lifetime. *Diego* is a natural choice to pair with Patricia Maloney Markun's *The Little Painter of Sabana Grande* (see page 84).

China

Alexander, Lloyd
The Remarkable Journey of Prince Jen
Dutton, 1991
Ages 10-14, 273 pp.
ISBN 0-525-44826-8 (hardcover)
   0-440-40890-3 (paperback—Dell/Yearling)

Chinese prince Jen bravely volunteers to search for the legendary kingdom of T'ien-kuo. All have heard of this fabled land and its marvels, but no one has actually set eyes upon them. Master Wu, a mysterious and ragged old man chooses six gifts for Prince Jen to carry with him: a saddle, a sword, a paint box, a bowl, a kite and a flute. Puzzled by the humbleness of the gifts but full of high spirits and pride, Jen sets off to discover the fabled kingdom. Perseverance in his quest teaches Jen the true meaning of the gifts, and he finally comes of age. A winner of numerous awards, including the American Library Association Best Children's Book, the book is filled with intricate and authentic details from Chinese culture.

Hong, Lily Toy
Two of Everything
Albert Whitman, 1993
Ages 4-8, unpaged
ISBN 0-8075-8157-7

When old Mr. Haktak finds a curious brass pot buried in his garden, he decides to bring it home for his wife to use in the kitchen. When Mrs. Haktak's hairpin falls into the pot, the old couple makes a startling discovery: everything that is tossed into the pot comes out doubled. After experimenting with replicating their few accumulated gold coins, Mrs. Haktak has an unfortunate accident and falls into the pot herself. Needless to say, a duplicate of his wife was not exactly at the top of Mr. Haktak's wish list, but the old couple manages to work out a wise resolution to the mishap. This whimsically illustrated tale will bring a smile to the face of readers, young and old alike.

Hong, Lily Toy
How the Ox Star Fell from Heaven
Albert Whitman, 1991
Ages 4-8, unpaged
ISBN 0-8075-3428-5

At the beginning of time, oxen did not exist on the earth. Swathed in silks, they lolled on cushiony clouds in heaven and never toiled at all. But, because life was hard for the folk on earth who often went for days without food, the Emperor of the Heavens sent the ox star down to earth to deliver his celestial decree that people should be able to eat at least once every three days. Unfortunately, the slow-witted ox star got the message mixed up and announced that the Emperor had decreed that people will eat three times a day, every day. Furious at this unexpected twist, the Emperor banishes the ox to earth where he becomes the farmer's beast of burden, ensuring that humanity may, indeed, eat three times a day.

Lee, Huy Voun
At the Beach
Henry Holt, 1994
Ages 5-10, unpaged
ISBN 0-8050-2768-8

During a break from splashing in the waves, Xiao Ming's mother amuses him by drawing Chinese characters in the sand with a stick. Through her illustrations of the sights to be seen during a day at the beach, artist Huy Voun Lee draws marvelous parallels between the Chinese pictographs and the concepts they represent. The character for sky flows into the flight of seagulls soaring through the air, while the depiction of the word "woman" looks like a mother contentedly holding her baby on the sand. The glossary and pronunciation guide on the book's endpapers further reinforce the similarity between some Chinese characters and the objects they represent. This beautiful and unusual picture book explores the uniqueness of the world's most widespread written language.

Louie, Ai-Ling
Yeh-Shen
Illustrated by Ed Young
Philomel Books, 1982
Ages 5-10, unpaged
ISBN 0-399-21594-8 (paperback)

The Cinderella story has deep roots in ancient Asia, where it has been found in texts dating back more than a thousand years before the tale emerged in the West. The heroine of the Chinese version is Yeh-Shen, daughter of a cave chief of southern China. The familiar stepmother and stepsister are here, as is a kindly uncle who makes it possible for Yeh-Shen to attend the spring festival banquet clad in a shimmering azure gown. Finding her diminutive golden slipper leads the determined king to search for its owner and, of course, we know how the story ends. The gentle storytelling style and misty illustrations accentuate the serenity of this version of the ancient tale.

Reddix, Valerie
Dragon Kite of the Autumn Moon
Illustrated by Jean and Mou-Sien Tseng
Lothrop, Lee & Shepard, 1991
Ages 4-8, unpaged
ISBN 0-688-11030-4

In the ninth month of every year, six days before the waxing of the full moon, the people of Taiwan celebrate Kite's Day. Tradition holds that when a kite is set free on the wind, it carries away with it all the misfortunes that might otherwise befall the owner. For as long as he can remember, young Tad-Tin has flown a special kite with his grandfather on Kite's Day, but this year his grandfather is ill and doesn't have the strength to make one for Tad-tin to set free. Tad-tin has only one kite to sacrifice—the beautiful dragon kite that Grandfather painstakingly crafted to celebrate his birth. This lovely story of a young child willing to give up a special treasure for the good of his grandfather will touch the hearts of young readers.

Schlein, Miriam
The Year of the Panda
Illustrated by Kam Mak
HarperTrophy, 1992
Ages 7-10, 83 pages
ISBN 0-06-440-366-1

Lu Yi and his family live on a farm in a remote, mountainous area of China. When Lu Yi finds a sick baby panda bear abandoned in the woods, he embarks on a journey of discovery about the endangered species. With the help of Dr. Di, a visiting American scientist, he learns about the efforts the Peking government is making to protect the panda population.

Yep, Laurence
The Rainbow People
HarperTrophy Paperbacks, 1992
Ages 8-14, 194 pp.
ISBN 0-06-440441-2

As a government-sponsored make-work project during the Great Depression, Chinese immigrants in Oakland, California, were interviewed and asked to recount the folktales they knew. Their stories were transcribed and translated, resulting in the creation of a treasure trove of traditional Chinese lore that had previously survived only by word of mouth. In this appealing collection, Laurence Yep retells 20 of these tales, including stories of tricksters and fools, love and loss, and the rocky earth and starry heavens.

Young, Ed
Lon Po Po
Philomel Books, 1989
Ages 4-10, unpaged
ISBN 0-399-21619-7

Three Chinese sisters are left at home alone when their mother visits their grandmother. Because she will be away overnight, Mother warns them to close the door and latch it tightly. A hungry old wolf who lives nearby notices the mother's departure and, disguising himself as the grandmother, tricks the girls into letting him into the house. Thought to be more than 1,000 years old, this Chinese tale of three young girls outwitting a nasty old wolf is reminiscent of the European tale,

Little Red Riding Hood. The distinctive pastel watercolor illustrations reminiscent of traditional Chinese panel painting lend the book a special charm. Winner of the Caldecott Medal.

Zhensun, Zheng & Alice Low
A Young Painter: The Life and Paintings of Wang Yani
Scholastic, 1991
Ages 8-14, 80 pp.
ISBN 0-590-44906-0

This unusual book examines the life and works of Wang Yani, a young girl from a small southern Chinese village who began painting when she was just a toddler. At the age of three, Yani astounded her artist father by picking up a paintbrush in his studio and producing beautiful drawings of monkeys and natural landscapes. A year later, one of her works was reproduced on a Chinese postage stamp. And, in 1989, when she had reached the ripe old age of 14, Yani had her first one-woman exhibition at the Smithsonian Institution in Washington, D.C. This book, by journalist Zhensun Zheng and art historian Alice Low, chronicles Yani's development as an artist, her life at home and while on tour, and her career aspirations. There is also an informative chapter on the tools and techniques used in Chinese brush painting. Liberally illustrated with a wide selection of Yani's work, the book also includes two fold-out spreads of her delicate scroll paintings.

Eastern Europe

Afanasyev, Alexander Nikolayevich
The Fool and the Fish
Retold by Lenny Hort
Illustrated by Gennady Spirin
Dial Books for Young Readers, 1990
Ages 4-8, unpaged
ISBN 0-8037-0861-0

Another in the rich tradition of the great fool stories from Russia, this is a clever retelling of a tale in which a lazy fool catches an enchanted fish that promises to make his every wish come true. At first, the fool uses the wishes only to dodge his chores but, as the plot thickens, he makes shrewder use of them than he would ever have imagined. Storyteller Alexander Nikolayevich Afanasyev occupies a place in Russian folk literature similar to Hans Christian Andersen in the West and is credited with introducing such outstanding characters as Baba Yaga the Witch and Vassilisa the Wise to Russian folklore. As always, Gennady Spirin's opulent and intricate illustrations capture the magic of the story. A *New York Times* Best-Illustrated Children's Book in 1990.

Ayres, Becky Hickox
Matreshka
Illustrated by Alexi Natchev
Doubleday Books for Young Readers, 1992
Ages 5-8, unpaged
ISBN 0-385-30657-1

When obedient young Kata receives a painted wooden Matreshka doll from a kind old lady, she simply slips it into her apron pocket and continues on her errand in the forest. When a bitter winter storm begins to swirl through the woods, however, Kata becomes lost and ends up a prisoner of the dreaded witch, Baba Yaga. It is then that the magical powers of Matreshka begin to reveal themselves. This tale based on Russian folklore complements the Hansel and Gretel story, which is more familiar to many children.

Brett, Jan
The Mitten
Putnam, 1989
Ages 4-8, unpaged
ISBN 0-399-21920-X

This is a very attractive adaptation of a cumulative Ukrainian folktale in which a young boy, Nicki, unknowingly loses one of the mittens his grandmother has knitted for him. One by one, woodland animals burrow into the lost mitten to keep warm until, finally, it is shot into the sky by the enormous sneeze of the bear, the last animal to squeeze in. Miraculously, the mitten finds its way back into Nicki's hands, and the last illustration shows us the puzzlement on the grandmother's face as she wonders how it could have stretched so much. The artwork is extraordinary, with each picture set into a decorative frame in the center of the page. The reader also sees Nicki in the borders of each page, walking through the woods, blithely unaware of what is going on.

Dolphin, Laurie
Georgia to Georgia: Making Friends in the U.S.S.R.
Photographs by E. Alan McGee
Tambourine Books, 1991
Ages 8-12, 32 pp.
ISBN 0-688-09896-7

Political realities have shifted since the publication of this book, which tells the story of the friendship mission of a young boy from Atlanta, Georgia, to Tbilisi, capital of the Soviet Republic of Georgia. The pictorial record of American Joe Schulten's journey to Georgia emphasizes modern family and school life in Georgia, including a trip to the local "Chess House" for a tournament and a glimpse of the classrooms and playing fields of Georgian schoolchildren, while also highlighting some of their ancient heritage and traditions.

Joe Schulten's mother founded the Atlanta-based Peace Tree Foundation, dedicated to helping American and Soviet children build bridges of friendship and understanding. Paata Shevardnadze states in her introduction, "The book...shows how satisfying understanding between people can be, particularly when this feeling is carried by children. Boys from two very distant Georgias, American and Soviet, became friends and opened up a totally new world."

Filipovic, Zlata
Zlata's Diary: A Child's Life in Sarajevo
Translated by Christina Pribichevich-Zoric
Viking, 1994
Ages 10 and up, 200 pp.
ISBN 0-670-85724-6

The weeks this book spent atop European and North American bestseller lists earned Zlata Filipovic celebrity as "Bosnia's Anne Frank." While 10-year-old Zlata's writing, even at its most piercing, will never equal the universal power of Anne Frank's work, her diary, nevertheless, provides us with a moving glimpse of the disintegration of Bosnia and a girl's longing for normal life. Excellent for use as a read-aloud or part of a diary study unit, *Zlata's Diary* focuses on the incomprehensibility of war as only the writing of a child can. As Zlata says, "I keep wanting to explain these stupid politics to myself, because it seems to me that politics caused this war, making it our everyday reality...It looks to me as though these politics mean Serbs, Croats and Muslims. But they are all people. They are all the same. They all look like people, there's no difference. They all have arms, legs and heads, they walk and talk, but now there's 'something' that wants to make them different."

Gogol, Nikolai
The Nose
Illustrated by Gennadij Spirin
David R. Godine, 1993
Ages 8-12, unpaged
ISBN 0-87923-963-8

In this fantastical story by the famous Russian writer, Nikolai Gogol, the reader is drawn into the surreal tale of a nose that disappears one morning from the face of a St. Petersburg civil servant and begins parading around the cathedrals and salons of the great Russian city in the guise of a fancy and fashionable military officer. After a series of misadventures that will entertain readers of all ages, the nose and its owner are finally reunited. The story is wonderfully illustrated with fanciful pictures of the nose in full military dress being drawn through the streets of the city in an open carriage or clad in a dashing cape, sweeping across great military plazas. Even the endpapers feature the nose in a wonderful braided tricorn hat. A good addition to folktale collections, this story can be appropriately geared to many age groups.

Kendall, Russ
Russian Girl: Life in an Old Russian Town
Scholastic, 1994
Ages 5-10, 40 pp.
ISBN 0-590-45789-6

Olga Surikova lives with her family in the 100-year-old Russia town of Suzdal, about 150 kilometers east of Moscow. This photographic essay is a pictorial description of Olga's life as a Grade 3 pupil in a traditional Russian school; as the granddaughter of a farm woman who strains her own milk and collects her own eggs; and as the daughter of a professional nurse who treats some children in her home, sometimes with the Russian folk medicine technique of "cupping." Building a snowman, losing a baby tooth or studying harder to get better marks in school, Olga's life may be very different from that of her North American counterparts, but her hopes, dreams, joys and fears are very much the same. Much useful information is contained in an extensive afterword, including the Cyrillic alphabet, a pronunciation guide for Russian words and several simple recipes. There are also brief background notes on the modern day economic travails of the average Russian family, which are reflected in this pictorial tour of Olga's daily life.

Kismaric, Carole
The Rumor of Pavel and Paali
Illustrated by Charles Mikolaycak
Harper and Row, 1988
Ages 5-10, unpaged
ISBN 0-06-023277-3

Twin brothers Pavel and Paali disagree over their basic philosophy of life. Kindly Paali believes that people profit most from doing good, while cynical Pavel maintains that it is only through evil and cunning that people can succeed. The two agree to a wager: if the first three people they ask agree with Paali, Pavel will give up all he owns to him; however, if they concur with Pavel, then Pavel will become owner of all Paali's worldly goods. When Pavel wins the bet, he holds Paali to his commitment. As the compassionate brother and his wife slowly starve, Pavel exacts an even heavier and more ruthless vengeance on his twin. But as cruelty often does, Pavel's misdeeds spark a chain of strange events that eventually lead to his demise. This powerful fable of the triumph of good over evil is a refreshing change from the many folktales on the same theme that are populated by imprisoned maidens and dashing young princes.

Langton, Jane
Salt: A Russian Folktale
Illustrated by Ilse Plume
Hyperion Books, 1992
Ages 6-10, unpaged
ISBN 1-56282-178-4

From a small Russian village, a father sends his three sons out into the world to seek their fortunes. Fyodor and Vasily, the two favored brothers, are sent off with ships full of precious cargo to barter, but Ivan, thought of by his father as a fool, is sent out in a small ship filled only with wooden spoons. While Fyodor and Vasily meet only misfortune, Ivan discovers a mountain made of salt—the spice of life—which he trades to a foreign *tsar* for barrels of gold and precious stones. Spurred on by his love for the beautiful *tsarevna* he meets on his journey, Ivan will not be stopped by any obstacle placed in his way by his greedy and resentful brothers.

Translated from a Russian folktale by Alexander Nikolayevich Afanasyev, the story of Ivan's bravery and generosity is a satisfying fairy tale.

Lerner Publications Staff
Ukraine Then and Now
Lerner Publications, 1993
Ages 10 and up, 64 pp.
ISBN 0-8225-2808-8

Prepared by a team of researchers, writers and photographers in the geography department of Lerner Publications, *Ukraine Then and Now* is one of the first books to portray Ukraine in its new role as a fully independent state. Ukraine gained its sovereignty from the Soviet Union on August 24, 1991. With an abundance of color photographs, maps and clearly written text, the book depicts Ukraine's geography, history, culture and society, as well as some of the challenges facing the new nation as it embarks on the road to democracy and participation in the global free market economy. *Ukraine Then and Now* is part of an entire series from Lerner on the new reality in former Soviet Socialist Republics. Other books focus on Armenia, Azerbaijan, Estonia, Georgia, Latvia, Lithuania and Uzbekistan.

Marton, Jirina
You Can Go Home Again
Annick Press, 1994
Ages 4-8, unpaged
ISBN 1-55037-991-7 (hardcover)
      1-55037-990-9 (paperback)

Annie has always enjoyed hearing stories of her mother's childhood in Prague. Now that freedom has come to her former country, Annie's mother has the opportunity to take her family with her to revisit the scenes and memories of her growing-up years. Although she no longer has any relatives living in Prague, Annie feels connected to her family's past in a palpable and moving way after she makes a surprising discovery during her stay. This book is based on author and illustrator Jirina Marton's poignant first journey back to her own homeland.

Moroney, Lynn
Elinda Who Danced in the Sky: An Estonian Folktale
Illustrated by Veg Reisberg
Children's Book Press, 1990
Ages 4-8, 32 pp.
ISBN 0-89239-066-2

Long ago, the lovely and kind-hearted Elinda was born from a tiny bird's egg. Her work was to direct the birds in their seasonal migrations and she tenderly dedicated herself to this task. Many celestial suitors came to seek her hand, but Elinda would go with no one until she met Prince Borealis, Lord of the Northern Lights. But the prince was so badly needed in his own kingdom that he could not return to earth to wed Elinda, whose delicate wedding veil can be seen to this day fluttering in the night sky as the Milky Way. This simply told *pourquoi* tale with bright illustrations will charm young listeners.

A good complement to this book is Jeanne M. Lee's *Legend of the Milky Way* (Henry Holt, 1982: ISBN 0-8050-1361-X—paperback), a similar tale from the Chinese tradition.

Pevear, Richard
Our King Has Horns!
Illustrated by Robert Rayevsky
Macmillan, 1987
Ages 4-8, unpaged
ISBN 0-02-773920-1

Reminiscent of *The Emperor's New Clothes*, this old Georgian tale stands the Hans Christian Andersen story on its ear by depicting the king as the only one who knows the secret of his real appearance, while his subjects remain ignorant; that is, until a barber of great repute is summoned to the court to cut the king's hair. While the king always banishes his hairstylists immediately after they discover the spiraling horns that he conceals under his crown, something about the diplomacy of this particular barber persuades the king to let him return to his people. The clever barber deals with his dangerous secret and manages to outwit the king in this amusing folktale about the persistent nature of the truth. Whimsical illustrations round out this appealing book.

Polacco, Patricia
Rechenka's Eggs
Philomel Books, 1988
Ages 4-8, unpaged
ISBN 0-399-21501-8

Old Babushka, renowned for her beautifully decorated eggs, is preparing her entries for this year's Easter Festival in old Moscow when she finds an injured goose that she nurses back to health. One day, Rechenka, the goose, accidentally overturns the basket containing Babushka's brilliantly painted eggs, breaking them all. But the miracle that greets Babushka the next morning is only the first of many that come to her as a result of the kindnesses she has heaped on Rechenka. A highlight of the illustrations is the wonderful reproductions of hand-painted Ukrainian Easter eggs, stemming from author-illustrator Patricia Polacco's own work as a decorator of these traditional objects.

Prochazkova, Iva
The Season of Secret Wishes
Translated by Elizabeth D. Crawford
Lothrop, Lee & Shepard, 1989
Ages 10-14, 214 pp.
ISBN 0-688-08735-3

Life in Prague just before the transition to democracy is beautifully described through the eyes of 11-year-old Kapka, the daughter of a Czech sculptor whose pieces have been deemed undesirable for inclusion in a government-sponsored art show. Kapka and her neighborhood friends rally around the desolate artist, and encourage him to mount a private street showing of his works. Although the street exhibition is a big success, an informer reports the event to the authorities who question and detain Kapka's father. While this book provides children with an introduction to a society in which free thought and expression are suppressed, Kapka's emotions and aspirations will be familiar to young people everywhere.

Sis, Peter
A Small Tall Tale from the Far Far North
Knopf, 1993
Ages 6-12, unpaged
ISBN 0-679-84345-0

One day in 1893, Czech folk hero Jan Welzl decided that he would set out overland across Siberia in the far North and East to find his fortune. When he could no longer travel by horse-drawn cart, he bartered them for reindeer and a sled and, after three long winters, he finally reached the Bering Sea. To this day, no one knows for sure whether Jan Welzl really existed or whether the stories about his legendary adventures are just tall tales. In this unusual picture book, author and illustrator Peter Sis has woven together all the information he could glean about Welzl's life with his own imaginings of what the odyssey must have been like. Maps, storyboards, dioramas, leaves from Welzl's imagined diaries and sketchbooks, and even a northern native myth told in pictographs unite to give the story a larger-than-life feeling.

Sis, Peter
The Three Golden Keys
Doubleday, 1994
Ages 6-12, unpaged
ISBN 0-385-47292-7

Prague's rich cultural history is magically evoked in this tale of a man who descends in a hot-air balloon to an ancient European town and discovers that he has returned to the city of his youth. An enchanted black cat leads the man on a journey around the beloved sites of his childhood and, at each stop, he receives a scroll imprinted with a traditional Czech legend about the city. Each of these is a tale in itself and, together, they weave a beautiful and mystical portrait of the old Czech capital. This book makes a wonderful springboard for encouraging both children and older readers to share stories of their own hometowns, as well as to research the stories behind the landmarks in the communities where they now live.

Trivas, Irene
Annie...Anya
Orchard Books, 1992
Ages 4-8, unpaged
ISBN 0-531-05452-7

When Annie's North American physician parents are invited to work in a Moscow hospital for a month, five-year-old Annie naturally joins them for this trip halfway around the world. Annie isn't enamored of Moscow at first, finding the churches too full of dark icons, the lines at the shops too long and the cartoons on television incomprehensible. With the one word of Russian she knows, she declares, "Russia is a big, fat NYET!" But when Annie starts daycare and befriends a little Russian girl coincidentally named Anya, her cold war with Russia begins to thaw. By trip's end, she is happily babbling away in Russian, and regretfully bidding *dosvidanye* to her best friend, Anya. Along with Ellen Levine's *I Hate English* (see page 26), this story can inspire a lively discussion of the difficulties of starting school in a new and unknown language.

UNICEF
I Dream of Peace
UNICEF/HarperCollins, 1994
Ages 8 and up, 80 pp.
ISBN 0-06-251128-9

The writings and drawings in this volume represent a step in the healing process experienced by just a few of the countless thousands of children whose lives were plunged into chaos and despair by the brutality of civil war in the former Yugoslavia. In many schools and refugee camps throughout the region, traumatized children were encouraged by teachers, psychologists and art therapists to work through the trauma they had undergone by expressing their feelings through words and pictures. As a fundraising project for its many refugee programs in war-torn areas around the world, UNICEF gathered some of the most moving prose, poems and full-color illustrations into this volume. With brief, moving introductions by children's author Maurice Sendak and UNICEF Executive Director James P. Grant, this book describes the horrors of war with both a lack of artifice and a hope for the future of which only children are capable.

Ushinsky, Constantin
How a Shirt Grew in the Field
Adapted by Marguerita Rudolph
Illustrated by Erica Weihs
Clarion Books, 1992
Ages 4-8, unpaged
ISBN 0-395-59761-7

Vasya's father keeps telling him that he is sowing seeds to grow shirts for Vasya and his baby sister, Anya. But Vasya doesn't understand how a shirt could poke its collar and sleeves straight up out of the black earth. As the seasons change, he watches the flax plants sprout and grow, and sees his older sisters pulling up the plants by the roots, drying the sheaves in the sun, and soaking them in the river. Over the winter, the process continues as family members card, spin, weave, bleach and embroider, until one day Vasya finally understands how a shirt can grow in the field. Although Constantin Ushinsky's simple tale of life in the Ukrainian countryside first appeared more than a century ago, it retains its appeal today. *How a Shirt Grew in the Field*, which lovingly details the way a shirt is produced, contrasts well with Phoebe Gilman's *Something from Nothing* (see page 123), which humorously recounts the demise of an article of clothing.

Vagin, Vladimir & Frank Asch
Here Comes the Cat!
Scholastic, 1989
Ages 3-8, unpaged
ISBN 0-590-41854-8

Russian illustrator Vladimir Vagin and American author and illustrator Frank Asch collaborated in a trans-Atlantic partnership to produce this book, the first to be designed by an American and painted by a Russian. A deceptively simple story builds suspense as a bilingual Russian and English mouse scurries through town and countryside, flying a balloon over an amusement park and diving underwater in the harbor to warn everyone that the cat is coming. The cat's climactic arrival, however, is not exactly what the reader anticipates. Beneath its humorous exterior, this whimsically illustrated book packs a powerful message about détente and friendship.

Winthrop, Elizabeth
Vasilissa the Beautiful
Illustrated by Alexander Koshkin
HarperCollins, 1991
Ages 5-10, 40 pp.
ISBN 0-06-021662-X (hardcover)
        0-06-443345-5 (paperback)

Every Russian child grows up with the tale of Vasilissa the Beautiful, also known as Vasilissa the Wise. In this retelling of the old fable, those familiar with Western fairy tale traditions will recognize elements of both *Cinderella* and *Hansel and Gretel*. After her mother's untimely death, Vasilissa must cope with her cruel stepmother and stepsisters, her only comfort the little doll her mother left her as a deathbed blessing. Her sisters send her to fetch fire from Baba Yaga, the witch in the forest, hoping she will never return. With the help of the magic doll, Vasilissa is able to conquer her fears of Baba Yaga and emerge unscathed. Russian illustrator Alexander Koshkin has supplied beautiful illustrations, including several two-page spreads depicting the 17th-century atmosphere that has become a tradition in Russian folktale illustration.

Rita Grauer's *Vasalisa and Her Magic Doll* (Philomel Books: ISBN 0-399-21986-2) is also a very satisfying retelling of this classic fairy tale, though the illustrations are not as breathtaking.

Wolkstein, Diane
Oom Razoom or Go I Know Not Where, Bring Back I Know Not What
Illustrated by Dennis McDermott
Morrow Junior Books, 1991
Ages 4-8, unpaged
ISBN 0-688-09416-3

Olga, the beautiful and talented wife of Alexis, the king's archer, weaves fabulous, priceless carpets. When the greedy king covets Olga for his own, he sends Alexis away on a seemingly impossible mission to Go I Know Not Where to Bring Back I Know Not What. But by dint of his own great generosity and with the help of the genie, Oom Razoom, Alexis attains the unattainable. Not only is he reunited with his wife, but he also becomes the new ruler of the kingdom.

The First Peoples of North America

Bruchac, Joseph
Fox Song
Illustrated by Paul Morin
Oxford University Press, 1993
Ages 5-9, unpaged
ISBN 0-19-541000-9

Laced with Native American respect for the land and all it holds, *Fox Song* is a gentle story of intergenerational love. Jamie and her great-grandmother, Grama Bowman, used to spend hours together walking in the woods, picking wild blackberries in the summer fields, and checking the sweetness of the early spring maple syrup. As Jamie comes to terms with the death of her beloved grandmother, she is comforted by memories of the old woman's wisdom about the special relationship between humans and nature, which is the heritage of the Abenaki people.

Caduto, Michael J. & Joseph Bruchac
The Native Stories from Keepers of the Earth
Fifth House Publishers, 1991
Ages 6 and up, 145 pp.
ISBN 0-920079-76-8

Gathered from First Nations groups all over North America, this collection of 24 stories concentrates on themes of people's everlasting relationship to earth. Through a variety of aboriginal creation stories, as well as sections on the eternal elements of fire, water, earth, wind and sky, and humankind's link to earth's other animals, the theme of searching for an equilibrium with the creatures and systems of our planet is developed and can teach us much about respecting our environment and our world. As native storyteller Joseph Bruchac writes in the introduction, "The knowledge that native people obtained from thousands of years of living and seeking balance, was, in a very real sense, quite scientific." In keeping with the aboriginal oral tradition, which really makes these stories come alive, Bruchac also recounts them on an audiocassette, available from the same publisher (ISBN 0-920079-86-5).

Dorris, Michael
Morning Girl
Hyperion, 1992
Ages 10-15, 74 pp.
ISBN 1-56282-284-5 (hardcover)
1-56282-661-1 (paperback)

In alternating chapters, Morning Girl, a 12-year-old Taino Indian, and her younger brother, Star Boy, vividly recreate their life on a Bahamian island in 1492. The sister, who loves to rise early, tells of seeing her reflection for the first time by looking into her father's eyes; of her mother's disappointment when her hopes for the healthy birth of her expected child are dashed; and of searching for blossoms to weave necklaces as a surprise for her parents. Star Boy, who loves to feel himself become one with the glitter of the night sky tells of being caught outside during a crashing hurricane and exploring the island with his best friend, Red Feathers. In Morning Girl's last narrative, she witnesses the arrival of the first Europeans to her world. Columbus and his men are "discovering" America, and Morning Girl optimistically thinks, "...we would find ways to get along together."

The dramatic epilogue of the book is a passage quoted from Columbus's diary, which reads in part, "...it seemed to me that they were a people poor in everything...They should be good and intelligent servants...and I believe that they would become Christians very easily, for it seems to me that they have no religion. Our Lord pleasing, at the time of my departure I will take six of them from here to Your Highnesses in order that they may learn to speak." With this ending, the eloquent voices of Morning Girl and Star Boy are silenced.

Goble, Paul
Love Flute
Bradbury Press, 1992
Ages 4-8, unpaged
ISBN 0-02-736261-2

Traditional courtship customs among the Plains Indians included the serenading of maidens by the young men with beautiful music played on a "love flute." Various myths explain the origin of the love flute, for, as Goble attests, "...men have always needed supernatural help to attract, and to keep, the women they love!" This gentle story of a shy young man in love with a much sought-after young woman, is one such sacred tale. Despairing when the object of his affections ignores him in favor of more high-profile suitors, the young hero retreats to the forest where the birds and animals give him a special gift to help him attract the young woman's attention and express his love in the only way he can. Paul Goble is an expert on ancient native lore whose careful research is evident in his many works for children.

Hausman, Gerald
Turtle Island ABC: A Gathering of Native American Symbols
Illustrated by Cara and Barry Moser
HarperCollins, 1994
Ages 5 and up, unpaged
ISBN 0-06-021308-6

Before Christopher Columbus arrived in North America, the land had been inhabited for thousands of years by tribes who referred to themselves as The People. They named the great land mass on which they lived Turtle Island, from ancient stories that were told of how the first turtle carried the land on her back. In this innovative alphabet book, each letter stands for an important symbol of North America's diverse native peoples, such as the eagle, the quartz stone and the yucca plant.
    Each entry comprises a short story, told in a quiet style evocative of the oral traditions of North America's first peoples. The hushed pastel illustrations accompanying each entry further contribute to the feeling of serenity and power created by the book.

Hobbs, Will
Bearstone
Avon Paperbacks, 1991
Ages 9-13, 154 pp.
ISBN 0-380-71249-0

Abandoned by his parents and living in a group home for native boys, 14-year-old Cloyd Atcitty is isolated, sullen and rebellious. When his housemother takes him to live for the summer with an elderly man in the Colorado mountains, Cloyd continues to act out his feelings of frustration and anger, even after he has begun to care deeply for for the old man. Through a precious second chance extended by the old man, Cloyd begins to learn how to reach out to those who offer him love—and how to return it. An exciting coming-of-age story, *Bearstone* combines adventure and vivid characterizations with a poignant, though never maudlin, description of the relationship between the boy and the old man. An American Library Association Best Book.

Hoyt-Goldsmith, Diane
Pueblo Storyteller
Photographs by Lawrence Migdale
Holiday House, 1991
Ages 8-12, 28 pp.
ISBN 0-8234-0864-7 (hardcover)
    0-8234-1080-3 (paperback)

Pueblo Storyteller paints a picture of the contemporary life of the native peoples of the American Southwest. April is a young native American girl who lives on the Cochiti Pueblo near Santa Fe, New Mexico. She speaks Keres, the language of the Cochiti tribe, as well as English. When April was a small child, her mother died, and she has lived with her grandparents in the pueblo ever since. Talented artisans, her grandparents are teaching April many of the traditional ways of her people, including baking bread in the outdoor oven known in Spanish as *horno*, and sculpting and painting the ancestral storyteller pottery figures.

Keegan, Marcia
Pueblo Boy: Growing Up in Two Worlds
Cobblehill Books, 1991
Ages 6-10, unpaged
ISBN 0-525-65060-1

While Diane Hoyt-Goldsmith's *Pueblo Storyteller* (see previous entry) focuses on the traditional artistry of the Pueblo Indians, *Pueblo Boy*, about 10-year-old Timmy of the Tewa tribe, provides readers with a glimpse of Pueblo spiritual life, dance ceremonies and ancient sites through the liberal use of large, color photographs. With its more detailed text and glossary, *Pueblo Storyteller* is a more satisfying book, but *Pueblo Boy* makes a good read-aloud introduction to Southwest Indian culture for younger readers.

Littlechild, George
This Land Is My Land
Children's Book Press, 1993
Ages 8 and up, 32 pp.
ISBN 0-89239-119-7

By presenting a unique collage of brightly colored paintings interspersed with wonderful old photographs of his ancestors, native Canadian artist George Littlechild reveals the experience of his people, the Plains Cree, as their way of life was destroyed by Canadians of European background. On a personal level, Littlechild documents his youth at boarding school, the difficult transition to an urban way of life so foreign to his heritage, and his discovery of self-expression through art. Underlying his personal reflections runs a current of pain caused by the wrongs committed against the native peoples of North America, which he knows must be righted in order to heal the wounds inflicted upon these nations.

London, Jonathan
Fire Race: A Karuk Coyote Tale
Illustrated by Sylvia Long
San Francisco Chronicle Books, 1993
Ages 5-9, unpaged
ISBN 0-8118-0241-8

The Karuk Indians of California have long handed down this tale of how humans learned to make fire by rubbing together brittle sticks of wood over dried mosses and grass. The wise old coyote, together with the help of his comrades the turtle, the lion, the eagle and the bear, decides to snatch some of the fire that the covetous yellow jacket bee sisters, sole possessors of the flame, have been hoarding in their cave up the mountainside. Leading the furiously buzzing insects on a high-speed chase, coyote wrests away some of the warm, bright flames and imbues the trees with the power to recreate fire's magic. Golden-hued illustrations enhance the fire theme, and some of the main animal characters wear traditional shell-and-beadwork necklaces, which are identified in an afterword. There is also a comprehensive bibliography listing sources of the myths and legends of the Karuk people.

Martin, Rafe
The Rough-Face Girl
Illustrated by David Shannon
Putnam, 1992
Ages 6-10, unpaged
ISBN 0-399-21859-9

In a village by the shores of Lake Ontario lived a very great, rich and powerful invisible being, who was also rumored to be handsome. However, no one was privileged to see this great invisible man except his sister, who zealously guarded him from the many young women who wished to marry him. No woman could be wed to him unless she could prove to his sister that she had actually seen him with her own eyes. This story is an Algonquin version of the Cinderella tale in which the rough-face girl, her face charred from years of hard work by the fire, tries to win the heart of the Invisible Being, after her beautiful, but cruel, sisters have failed. An excellent addition to a cross-cultural fairy tale theme, this traditional story focuses on the rewards that will ultimately come to those who are good and kind.

Rhoads, Dorothy
The Corn Grows Ripe
Puffin Paperbacks, 1993
Ages 8-12, 88 pp.
ISBN 0-14-036313-0

A happy but often irresponsible 12-year-old Yucatan boy, Tigre must suddenly grow up when his father is seriously hurt in an accident. Though Tigre has never before done a man's work, he bravely embarks upon the task of clearing and burning the family's new corn field, a ritualized duty that dates back to ancient Mayan times. A touching coming-of-age story, this novel, originally published in 1956, skilfully links the sacred crop—corn—with the lives and beliefs of the Mayan people.

Roop, Peter & Connie Roop
Ahyoka and the Talking Leaves
Illustrated by Yoshi Miyake
Beech Tree Paperbacks, 1994
Ages 7-10, 60 pp.
ISBN 0-688-133082-8

This is a fictionalized account of the famous Cherokee, Sequoyah, the first person to create an entire written alphabet and language from a spoken one. His young daughter, Ahyoka, which means "she who brought happiness," helps him in the long and arduous process of developing a syllabary encoding all the sounds of the Cherokee language into 86 characters. The alphabet was adopted by the Cherokee people in 1821, and within a year, most Cherokees were reading and writing in their own language. In 1828, the first Cherokee-language newspaper was published, thanks to the amazing accomplishment of Sequoyah and Ahyoka. An excellent resource to use along with this book is Leonard Everett Fisher's *Alphabet Art: Thirteen ABCs from Around the World* (see page 159), which includes large reproductions of the full Cherokee alphabet.

Seymour, Tryntje Van Ness
The Gift of Changing Woman
Illustrated with paintings by Apache artists
Henry Holt, 1993
Ages 10 and up, 38 pp.
ISBN 0-8050-2577-4

As an honored guest at an Apache Changing Woman ceremony in Arizona, Tryntje Van Ness Seymour was struck by the profound power of this ancient native ritual and inspired to share her experiences by writing a book. The well-researched result describes the traditional coming-of-age ceremony for young Apache women, in which they use special dances and prayers to re-enact the Apache story of creation and celebrate the power of Changing Woman, the legendary ancestor of their people. Interviews with an Apache medicine man, a father of several children, and a woman who experienced the ceremony years ago, are spliced together with a detailed informational narrative outlining each aspect of the sacred four-day ritual. Paintings gathered from a number of museum collections in the American Southwest present the ritual, called the *Na'ii'ees* ceremony, through the eyes of 19th- and 20th-century Apache artists. This thoughtful book is an exemplary attempt to present an authentic aspect of native American culture through their own voices and eyes.

Taylor, C.J.
How Two-Feather Was Saved from Loneliness: An Abenaki Legend
Tundra Books, 1990
Ages 4-8, unpaged
ISBN 0-88776-254-9

Long ago, a man named Two-Feather lived alone, subsisting on bark and roots and despairing of his loneliness. One day, he is awakened from a nap by the soft voice of a woman who promises she will lead him out of solitude forever. He follows the silken-haired spirit to a clearing where she is transformed into the first stalk of corn on earth. Two-Feather learns to cultivate the corn and, as other people are attracted to his field, a settlement grows up. He never knows loneliness again. Taylor's most recent book is *How We Saw the World: Nine Native Stories of the Way Things Began* (Tundra Books, 1993: ISBN 0-88776-302-2).

Japan

Akio, Terumasa
Me and Alves: A Japanese Journey
Illustrated by Yuriko Oido
Annick Press, 1993
Ages 5-8, unpaged
ISBN 1-55037-222-X paperback

Alves, an exchange student from Brazil, journeys to Japan and is billeted with a farming family on Hokkaido, Japan's northern island. He works in the fields, goes to the village festivals, wins a sumo wrestling competition and visits the local school to talk about life in his homeland. The author is the founder of an international exchange program that has brought thousands of foreign students to Japan and helped break down stereotypes about *gaijin* (non-Japanese).

Coerr, Eleanor
Mieko and the Fifth Treasure
Putnam, 1993
Ages 8-12, 80 pp.
ISBN 0-399-22434-3 (hardcover)
      0-440-40947-0 (paperback—Dell Yearling)

Calligraphy is the most important thing in 10-year-old Mieko's life. Along with the four tangible treasures needed to paint graceful word pictures—a fine sable brush, an inkstick, an inkstone shaped like a lily pond, and a roll of Japanese rice paper—Mieko also possesses what her art teacher describes as the "fifth treasure": the talent and artistic vision to make her calligraphy come alive and touch people's hearts with its grace and beauty. Everything suddenly changes, however, on the August day in 1945 when the atom bomb is dropped on Nagasaki. Mieko's right hand is so seriously slashed by a shard of flying glass that she can't begin to think of trying to lift a paintbrush, and she loses all confidence in her ability to practice her beloved art.

When Mieko is sent to her grandparents' village to live and asked to enter a calligraphy competition in the school, she has a chance to learn a valuable lesson about the true meaning of the fifth treasure. The title of each chapter of this beautifully told story of courage is presented in harmonious calligraphy, and there is also a short afterword explaining the techniques of calligraphic art.

Coerr, Eleanor
Sadako and the Thousand Paper Cranes
Illustrated by Ronald Himler
Dell Paperbacks, 1977
Ages 8-12, 64 pp.
ISBN 0-440-47465-5 (hardcover)

This powerful classic tells of Sadako Sasaki's tragic struggle with leukemia, a disease that killed—and continues to kill—thousands of people who survived the atomic bomb explosion over Hiroshima on August 6, 1945. Sasaki died in 1955 at the age of 12. While hospitalized, she had begun folding paper cranes in the naive hope that if she made 1,000, a miracle would occur. She made 644 of the origami birds before succumbing. Her classmates finished the last 356 in tribute. In 1958, a statue of Sasaki holding a golden crane was unveiled at the Hiroshima Peace Park. Today, members of the Folded Crane Club place thousands of paper birds beneath the statue on August 6, Peace Day. Their wish is engraved on the statue's pedestal: "This is our cry, this is our prayer, peace in the world."

Coerr, Eleanor
Sadako
Illustrated by Ed Young
Putnam, 1993
All ages, 48 pp.
ISBN 0-399-21771-1

A decade and a half after *Sadako and the Thousand Paper Cranes* (see previous entry) appeared, Sadako's story was made into a film. Caldecott Medal-winning artist Ed Young was chosen to do the soft pastel illustrations of the brave Japanese girl for the film. A selection of these images has been collated into a picture book and combined with an abridged version of the story by Eleanor Coerr, giving younger children access to Sadako's story for the first time. The award-winning half-hour video is distributed by Informed Democracy, P.O. Box 67, Santa Cruz, California 95063 (1-800-827-0949).

Godden, Rumer
Great Grandfather's House
Illustrated by Valerie Littlewood
Greenwillow Books, 1992
Ages 7-10, 76 pp.
ISBN 0-688-11319-2
   0-09-925491-3 (paperback—Red Fox)

Having lived in the big city all her young life, Keiko does not want to spend three months in the country with her great-grandfather while her parents are away in England. But she has no choice and, after a long train ride and ferryboat crossing, she arrives at Great Grandfather's long, low house. Its small rooms are divided by sliding paper screens and there are no chairs, only cushions on the floor. Adjusting to a completely different way of life that adheres to old traditions is not easy for a spoiled and independent city child like Keiko, who is used to getting her own way. Nevertheless, when her parents arrive to take her back to the city, Keiko finds herself tearful at the prospect of leaving the people and place she has come to love. This softly written story is an excellent read-aloud for younger children.

Higa, Tomiko
The Girl with the White Flag
Translated by Dorothy Britton
Dell Paperbacks, 1991
Ages 10-16, 128 pp.
ISBN 0-440-40720-6

In this poignantly graphic memoir, Tomiko Higa tells how she survived as a seven-year old wandering alone on the battlefields of Okinawa, Japan, at the end of World War II. Searching for her lost sisters, the orphaned Tomiko subsisted by scavenging food from the knapsacks of dead soldiers and seeking shelter in caves. On June 25, 1945, her ordeal came to an end. John Hendrickson, a U.S. Army signal corps photographer capturing images of Japanese soldiers surrendering, snapped a memorable picture of her—barefoot and in tattered clothes, waving a white piece of cloth tied to a crooked stick. Nearly 35 years later, the two met in Texas in a cathartic reunion. This story of the Imperial Army's desperate defense of the island of Okinawa, as seen through the eyes of a young girl, makes a powerful statement about the horror of war.

Ishii, Momoko
The Tongue-Cut Sparrow
Translated by Katherine Paterson
Illustrated by Suekichi Akaba
Lodestar, 1987
Ages 4-8, 40 pp.
ISBN 0-5256-7199-4

In this retelling of the Japanese version of a universal folktale, a kindly old man befriends a sparrow. His greedy and mean-spirited wife, however, cuts out the bird's tongue. The elderly man seeks out the sparrow to apologize and is richly rewarded, while his wife is taught the error of her ways. One charming feature of this book is the retention of some of the original Japanese onomatopoeic words, such as *gosho gosho*, the sound of water sloshing, and *chun chun*, the chirping of a sparrow. Stylized and droll brush drawings complement the text, suggesting the influence of classic Japanese scroll work.

Levine, Arthur A.
The Boy Who Drew Cats: A Japanese Folktale
Illustrated by Frederic Clement
Dial Books, 1993
Ages 6-10, unpaged
ISBN 0-8037-1172-7

In Kenji's drawings, flowers bloom, rivers flow, goldfish swim and cats seem to leap to life. But for all his artistic talent, frail Kenji cannot survive on his family's farm. Sent to live at the village monastery, he is soon expelled for drawing pictures when he should have been studying. Kenji begins wandering, encountering many perils along the way. Then, one heart-stopping night, he discovers a power to his art that helps him overcome the dangers lurking in the dark. The misty illustrations of menacing spirits are embellished by the stares of partially hidden cats that almost become part of the landscape in this atmospheric retelling of an old Japanese legend.

Mori, Kyoko
Shizuko's Daughter
Fawcett/Juniper Paperbacks, 1993
Ages 14 and up, 214 pp.
ISBN 0-449-70433-5

Shizuko Okuda turned on the gas in her kitchen in Kobe, Japan, one day and committed suicide. Only 12 years old, her daughter, Yuki, must now learn to live with a distant, taciturn father and his new wife, who embodies the stereotype of the cold, cruel stepmother. Living in a spotless and unfeeling home with only the memory of her mother, Yuki tries to make sense of a tragedy that made no sense at all. Kyoko Mori's understated prose is a powerful stylistic device that enhances the stifling sense of isolation Yuki feels. An American Library Association Best Book for Young Adults in 1994.

Nomura, Takaaki
Grandpa's Town
Kane/Miller Book Publishers, 1991
Ages 4-8, unpaged
ISBN 0-916291-36-7

Originally published in Japan in 1989, this bilingual Japanese and English version of *Grandpa's Town* was produced by Kane/Miller Book Publishers of New York, an innovative firm in the American multicultural book industry. Tome, a young Japanese boy, goes to stay with his recently widowed grandfather in his rural Japanese village. Tome and his mother assume that Grandpa must be very lonely and try to persuade him to move to the city and live with them. One day, though, when Tome visits the public bath with his grandfather, he realizes that he is not as lonely as he thought. In the town where he has lived all his life, Grandpa is surrounded by his friends and neighbors. This appealing story also provides an interesting look at the tradition of the Japanese public bath house.

San Souci, Robert D.
The Samurai's Daughter
Illustrated by Stephen D. Johnson
Dial Books for Young Readers, 1992
Ages 4-8, unpaged
ISBN 0-8037-1135-2

Inspired by a medieval Japanese legend and embellished with details from other Japanese folklore, this is a tale of Tokoyo, the brave daughter of a *samurai* nobleman. When the king banishes Tokoyo's father to the remote Oki Islands off Japan's western coast, she decides to attempt to free him from exile. Tokoyo has spent her childhood learning the art of the *amas*, hardy women sea divers who harvest oysters and other shellfish from the sea bed. Her diving skill, along with her courage and determination, prove to be Tokoyo's best weapons in her struggle to be reunited with her father. This story makes a welcome addition to the ranks of children's folklore stories that portray women in strong roles.

Say, Allen
Tree of Cranes
Houghton Mifflin, 1991
Ages 4-8, 32 pp.
ISBN 0-395-52024-X

The narrator, a young boy in Japan, is introduced to Christmas by his American-born mother, as she decorates a pine tree with a raft of folded paper cranes. This quietly told story subtly intimates that we are all products of the overlapping combination of diverse cultures. The illustrations, also by the author, show authentic details of Japanese home life.

Shute, Linda
Momotaro the Peach Boy
Lothrop, Lee & Shepard, 1986
Ages 5-8, unpaged
ISBN 0-688-05863-9

This Japanese legend tells of a boy found floating inside a giant peach by a kindly but childless old couple. Named Momotaro—the Peach Boy—he grows up to fight and vanquish the terrible demons that have terrorized his village for years. Retold and illustrated by

Linda Shute, the fable originated centuries ago. In 1868, when education for children became compulsory in Japan, the story was adapted for a government-compiled textbook. In this way, the oral tradition was standardized and *Momotaro* became one of the most popular folktales in Japan today.

Snyder, Dianne
The Boy of the Three-Year Nap
Illustrated by Allen Say
Houghton Mifflin, 1988
Ages 5-10, 32 pp.
ISBN 0-395-44090-4 (hardcover)
  0-395-66957-X (paperback)

Taro, the son of an industrious widow, is the laziest boy in all Japan. It was said that if no one woke him, he would sleep three years at a stretch. In this beautifully illustrated trickster tale, Taro hatches a plot to marry a rich merchant's daughter, thus ensuring that his naptime will never be disturbed. But he hasn't reckoned with his clever mother, who outwits him, and fixes things so that Taro will have a happy but hardworking future.

Younger children will love hearing this story read aloud, while older students will enjoy it as part of a study of folktales. And everyone will feast their eyes on the vibrantly colored Japanese-style brush line drawings of this Caldecott Honor book.

Tompert, Ann
Bamboo Hats and a Rice Cake
Illustrated by Demi
Crown Publishers, 1993
Ages 6-10, unpaged
ISBN 0-517-59272

Characters from the Japanese writing system are woven into the text of this charming story, an adaptation of a traditional folktale about a poor old man who goes to town to buy rice cakes for the New Year. As he encounters others who are even worse off than he, he becomes entangled in a series of negotiations. Japanese calligraphic characters replace the English text for words such as kimono, rice cake and bamboo hat. This poses no problem, however, as a glossary in Japanese and English is presented with beautiful simplicity on each page. The book contains some interesting lessons in comparative linguistics for children who will learn, for example, that Japanese doesn't distinguish between the singular and plural forms of words: the correct form must be discerned through context clues. Endnotes on the importance of New Year's celebrations and the pervasiveness of rice in Japanese culture supply even more insights.

Watkins, Yoko Kawashima
So Far from the Bamboo Grove
Puffin Paperbacks, 1986
Ages 10-14, 183 pp.
ISBN 0-14-032385-6

A harrowing account of a desperate flight, this is the fictionalized autobiography of the author, a young Japanese girl living with her family in Korea at the end of World War II. Once firmly ensconced as members of the ruling regime, Yoko's family becomes refugees fleeing the advancing North Korean army when the defeat of the Japanese turns the tables. Running for their lives at night, squeezing into railway cars, searching for food and shelter, and scratching messages on train station walls in the hope that her brother will find them, Yoko, her sister and mother make their agonizing way back to Japan. An American Library Association Notable Book, this novel can be compared with Sook Nyul Choi's *Year of Impossible Goodbyes* (see page 130), which tells a similar story from a very different perspective.

In the sequel, *My Brother, My Sister and I* (Bradbury Press, 1994: ISBN 0-02-792526-9), 13-year-old Yoko and her older brother and sister try to locate their still-missing father while enduring the harsh living conditions of post-war Japan.

Watkins, Yoko Kawashima
Tales from the Bamboo Grove
Illustrated by Jean & Mou-sien Tseng
Bradbury Press, 1992
Ages 8-14, 49 pp.
ISBN 0-02-792525-0

In this book, Yoko Kawashima Watkins has put together a collection of Japanese folktales recalled from her childhood. Each short tale is illustrated with a full-page ink-and-brush drawing that includes the story's title in Japanese calligraphy.

Wells, Ruth
A to Zen: A Book of Japanese Culture
Illustrated by Yoshi
Picture Book Studio, 1992
Ages 6-12, 24 pp.
ISBN 0-88708-175-4

A to Zen is more than a conventional alphabet book. Set up in the style of a Japanese book, it opens from back to front—from the perspective of native English speakers. The heading on each page is also set out in Japanese as it is read downward from the top right corner. And, because Japanese has no sounds equivalent to those represented by the English letters L, Q, V and X, the book contains only 22 topic words. Young readers are introduced to ancient Japanese traditions such as *aikido*, a martial art form, the *bunraku* puppet theater, and *chanoyu*, the graceful tea ceremony. Balancing these traditional concepts are aspects of contemporary young people's lives, such as *janken*, a finger-play game, *pachinko*, a Japanese version of pinball, and *wokuman*, the electronic brainchild of a company called Sony.

Yagawa, Sumiko
The Crane Wife
Translated by Katherine Paterson
Illustrated by Suekichi Akaba
Mulberry Books, 1987
Ages 5-9, 32 pp.
ISBN 0-688-07048-5 (paperback)

The Crane Wife is among Japan's most beloved folktales and has been made into movies, plays and even an opera. After the hero, Yohei, a poor farmer, saves a crane whose wing has been pierced by an arrow, a beautiful but mysterious young woman begs to become his wife. Three times she weaves for him an exquisite bolt of silken fabric. But Yohei is unable to heed his wife's request not to look in on her as she is working—with tragic results. The graceful illustrations in this book are haunting in their simplicity.

The Jewish Experience

Bachrach, Susan D.
Tell Them We Remember: The Story of the Holocaust
Little, Brown, 1994
Ages 10-16, 112 pp.
ISBN 0-316-07484-5 (paperback)

The most compelling historical account of the Nazi Holocaust available for young readers today, this book is an essential companion to the study of children's Holocaust literature. *Tell Them We Remember* provides an excellent and concise chronological account of the Nazi's persecution and extermination of the Jews, with well-written sections on the institutionalization of anti-Semitism across the Third Reich, the death camps that comprised the "Final Solution," and the courageous resistance and rescue operations that tragically saved all too few Jews from annihilation. Hitler's oppression of Gypsies, Poles, Jehovah's Witnesses, and the mentally and physically handicapped is also addressed. But what sets this book apart from other Holocaust histories is its use of photos and stories of 20 children and youths who were caught up in the maelstrom of Nazi Europe. As their stories unfold, they are intertwined with the historical text, and readers don't know until the end of the book which of them perished and which survived.

Tell Them We Remember was produced by the United States Holocaust Memorial Museum in Washington, D.C., where the identity card project from which the biographies were drawn is an integral part of the visitor's experience at the museum.

Cohen, Barbara
The Carp in the Bathtub
Illustrated by Joan Halpern
Kar-Ben Copies, 1972
Ages 6-10, 32 pp.
ISBN 0-930494-67-9

With the Jewish holiday of Passover fast approaching, Brooklyn brother and sister Harry and Leah befriend the bright-eyed carp temporarily living in their apartment bathtub. They hatch a plan to rescue him from their mother, who is about to turn him into a succulent plate of gefilte fish to grace the Passover table. The friendship of Leah and Harry with Joe, the carp, and their struggle to save him from the chopping knife is a Jewish classic, told with a bittersweet and gently humorous edge.

Cohen, Barbara
Molly's Pilgrim
Illustrated by Michael J. Deraney
Dell Paperbacks, 1983
Ages 6-10, 42 pp.
ISBN 0-440-41057-6

It is the early 20th century in a small American town, not yet used to playing host to new immigrants. The girls in Molly's third-grade class make fun of her accented English and laugh at her old-country ways. Molly wants to go back to Russia, until her mother reminds her that they have come to America to flee religious persecution at the hands of the Cossacks. Then, when Molly participates in a Thanksgiving project, she and her classmates come to realize that "it takes all kinds of Pilgrims to make a Thanksgiving." Reissued in 1995, *Molly's Pilgrim* was also made into an Academy Award-winning short film.

A companion to *Molly's Pilgrim*, *Make a Wish, Molly* (Doubleday, 1994: ISBN 0-385-31079-X) recounts what happens when Molly is invited to a friend's birthday party on Passover and cannot sample the cake because it's baked with yeast.

Cohen, Barbara
Yussel's Prayer
Illustrated by Michael J. Deraney
Mulberry Paperbacks, 1993
Ages 4-8, unpaged
ISBN 0-688-04581-2

In a small synagogue in turn-of-the-century Eastern Europe, all the townspeople are assembled to ask God's forgiveness on Yom Kippur. Everyone is there except Yussel, the illiterate young farmhand who sleeps in wealthy Reb Meir's barn. As they pray, the minds of the villagers begin to wander as they ruminate on their business and social ambitions. They become impatient as the long day of fasting and contemplation nears its end, but the wise Rabbi feels that he cannot end the service until someone gives thanks honestly for God's great gifts. This finally happens in the form of a truly pious and special contribution from Yussel, the cowherd. This gentle story gives young readers a real feeling for the spirit and meaning of this holiest Jewish day.

Drucker, Olga Levy
Kindertransport
Henry Holt, 1992
Ages 10-14, 148 pp.
ISBN 0-8050-1711-9

Olga Levy was born in Stuttgart in 1927, when Jews were an integral part of German society. Her father, a decorated World War I veteran of the German army, was a prosperous and influential book publisher, and her family lived a comfortable and intellectually stimulating life.

But on November 9, 1938—*Kristallnacht*, the "night of the broken glass"—Olga's parents saw the writing on the wall for Jews in the Third Reich. They arranged for Olga to be part of the Kindertransport operation, in which 10,000 German Jewish children were sent by train to England. This was a foreign land where the evacuees knew no one, spoke not a word of the language, and worried constantly about the fate of their families. In this powerful autobiography, Olga Levy Drucker describes her evacuation and her experiences as a young girl during the six difficult war years, a little-known chapter in Holocaust history.

Gilman, Phoebe
Something from Nothing
Scholastic, 1992
Ages 4-8, unpaged
ISBN 0-590-73802-X

Phoebe Gilman has created a whimsical artistic gem in her retelling of this simple Eastern European Jewish folktale. Over the years, Joseph's blanket, sewn for him by his grandfather when he was just a baby, becomes worn and frayed. Over the seasons, it is cut down more and more—into a jacket, a vest, a tie, a handkerchief and, finally, a colorful button. In the end, there is just enough fabric left to inspire Joseph to write a wonderful story, which will be with him always.

The real magic of this book, however, lies in Gilman's illustrations, a story in themselves. Every time Joseph's blanket is cut down and the remnants discarded, a band of mice living underneath the family home reaps a bonanza. Over the years, the industrious mouse family sews an entire wardrobe of clothing, as well as linens, curtains and upholstery for their comfortable rodent abode. Humorous artistic touches abound, right down to the illustration on the last page in which Joseph proudly shows his family his story with the tiny title written in authentic Yiddish text. Named to many "best" and "choice" lists, *Something from Nothing* won the Governor General's Award for children's literature in Canada.

Greenfeld, Howard
The Hidden Children
Ticknor and Fields, 1993
Ages 10 and up, 118 pp.
ISBN 0-395-66074-2

During World War II, thousands of Jewish children were spirited away from their homes and hidden from the Nazis. Most of them lived with strangers who risked their own lives to save them. They were hidden in convents and orphanages, in haylofts and underground passages, and in attics and basements. Some were well-looked-after, others suffered cruel abuse, but all were robbed of their childhoods. Even the youngest learned to lie, conceal their true identities and deny their religion. They learned to remain silent, knowing that to laugh, cry or speak loudly at the wrong time would endanger their lives and those of their protectors.

In this book, Howard Greenfeld interweaves the experiences of 13 of these children to create a compelling story that juxtaposes selfless sacrifice with humans' terrible inhumanity to humans. Illustrated with photographs of the children taken during the period of hiding, this book was an American Library Association Notable Children's Book, as well as an International Reading Association Best Book for 1994.

Hesse, Karen
Letters from Rivka
Henry Holt, 1992
Ages 8-14, 148 pp.
ISBN 0-8050-1964-2 (hardcover)
     0-14-036391-2 (paperback—Puffin)

Winner of numerous honors, including the 1992 Christopher Medal and the National Jewish Book Award, this diary-style story recounts the arduous journey of Russian Jewish immigrants to a better life in the United States. In letters to her young cousin back home, Rivka chronicles her family's flight from Russia in 1919. When the family finally arrives in Belgium, Rivka has an illness that prevents her from boarding the ship to America and she must remain alone in Antwerp until she can join her parents in New York. Based on a true story from the author's family, *Letters from Rivka* is a gripping depiction of the Jewish immigrant experience in the early years of the 20th century.

Hirsh, Marilyn
Joseph Who Loved the Sabbath
Illustrated by Davis Grebu
Viking Kestrel, 1986
Ages 3-8, unpaged
ISBN 0-670-81194-7 (hardcover)
     0-14-050670-5 (paperback—Puffin)

Suggested by a brief passage in the Talmud, the multifaceted Jewish compendium of Biblical lore and law, this story tells of a devout farmworker, Joseph, who toils all week in the fields of his wealthy master, Sorab. To honor the Sabbath, Joseph always lavishes his meager earnings on the choicest oil, wine, flour and chickens. One night, the greedy Sorab dreams that Joseph will take over all his lands and riches. Frightened, Sorab sells his possessions, uses the wealth to buy a giant ruby, and flees, trying to put as much distance as possible between himself and Joseph. But the fate of the good and pious can't be so easily thwarted, as the dénouement of this story shows young readers.

Leitner, Isabella
The Big Lie
Scholastic, 1992
Ages 9-14, 80 pp.
ISBN 0-590-45569-9 (hardcover)
0-590-45570-2 (paperback)

In this searing memoir, Isabella Leitner tells how she survived incarceration in the shadow of the crematoria at Auschwitz, as well as a death march into Germany under the guns of the retreating German army. An excellent introduction to the Holocaust for young readers, the book is simply, yet eloquently, written. Teachers and librarians should be aware that Leitner does not mince words about the unspeakable mass murder that took place in the gas chambers of Auschwitz. With its simple prose that, nevertheless, makes a complex statement about the nature of human evil, *The Big Lie* is excellent for use with both adolescent and adult ESL students.

Lowry, Lois
Number the Stars
Dell Paperbacks, 1991
Ages 9-12, 137 pp.
ISBN 0-440-80291-1

In October 1943, the occupying Nazis forces planned to deport all the Jews of Denmark to death camps. However, the Jewish community and Danish resistance leaders got wind of the plan and nearly 7,000 Jews—virtually the entire Jewish population of Denmark—were spirited across the sea to freedom in Sweden. A suspenseful story that builds to a tension-filled climax, *Number the Stars* tells how 10-year-old Annemarie Johansen and her family help her Jewish best friend, Ellen Rosen, and her family escape. Annemarie learns that courage means carrying on in the face of danger when you are doing something you believe in. The 1990 winner of the Newbery Award.

Matas, Carol
Sworn Enemies
Dell/Laurel Leaf Paperbacks, 1993
Ages 12-16, 132 pp.
ISBN 0-440-21900-0

Set in Odessa, Russia, in the mid-19th century, this suspenseful tale of morality and revenge pits two Jewish youths, Aaron and Zev, against each other. At the time, Jews were forcibly conscripted into the Tzar's army and baptized as Christians, in the hope that they would assimilate and Russia's Jewish population would dwindle. Each Jewish community was required to fill an annual conscription quota and, when not enough boys could be found, the Jewish authorities hired *khappers*, professional kidnappers, to round up the necessary bodies. Zev, a Jewish *khapper*, captures Aaron and delivers him to the Russian forces but, by a trick of fate, he, too, ends up in the clutches of the Russian troops. The narration alternates between Aaron and Zev, as each boy learns to deal with the humiliations heaped upon him by his sergeants, and to cope with the ultimate shame of forcible conversion to Christianity. *Sworn Enemies* provides a provocative catalyst for discussion of the universal themes of vengeance and forgiveness. An American Library Association Best Book for Young Adults in 1994.

Oberman, Sheldon
The Always Prayer Shawl
Illustrated by Ted Lewin
Boyds Mills Press, 1994
Ages 6-9, unpaged
ISBN 1-878093-22-3

This quiet story focuses on the comforting link to the identity of past generations that a special traditional object can provide. A prayer shawl is carried from Russia to America in the early 20th century and handed down from father to son to grandson, a symbol of constancy in the changes that engulf our lives. Winner of the 1994 National Jewish Book Award for Children's Picture Books.

Polacco, Patricia
Tikvah Means Hope
Doubleday, 1994
Ages 4-10, unpaged
ISBN 0-385-32059-0

With the devastating 1992 fire in the hillside residential areas of Oakland, California, as a backdrop, Patricia Polacco has created a bittersweet story of the hope that can rise from the ashes of destruction. Two neighborhood children, Justine and Duane, help their elderly friend, Mr. Roth, build his Sukkah, the open-roofed wooden booth, decorated with branches and fruit, that Jews build to celebrate the harvest thanksgiving holiday of Sukkot. After the firestorm rages through the hills, destroying thousands of homes and leaving more than two dozen people dead, the neighbors, still in shock, sort through the rubble that is all that's left their lives. The one spot of joy in this catastrophe is that somehow both Mr. Roth's Sukkah and his beloved cat, Tikvah, have emerged unscathed. Woven into this poignant, multicultural story is the important theme of the links that exist across generations.

Rosen, Michael J.
Elijah's Angel
Illustrated by Aminah Brenda Lynn Robinson
Harcourt Brace, 1992
Ages 5-8, unpaged
ISBN 0-15-225394-7

Both the author and illustrator of this story grew up in the neighborhood of Columbus, Ohio, where Elijah Pierce, a barber, woodcutter and son of a slave, ran a haircutting establishment for more than half a century. In the book, Michael is a nine-year-old Jewish boy who likes to visit Elijah's barber shop and listen to the old man's stories as he trims hair surrounded by the hundreds of carvings he has crafted over the decades. When Elijah shows his affection for Michael by giving him a carved angel for Christmas, Michael is worried that the forbidden "graven image" will desecrate his Jewish home. But Michael's parents help him understand the universal message of Elijah's gift, and the young boy reciprocates by giving Elijah a handmade Hanukkah menorah for the holiday candles. The realistic and non-syrupy message of intergenerational and interfaith understanding won this book the National

Jewish Book Award for a children's picture book in 1993.

van der Rol, Ruud & Rian Verhoeven
Anne Frank—Beyond the Diary: A Photographic Remembrance
Viking, 1993
Ages 10 and up, 116 pp.
ISBN 0-670-84932-4

This photobiography was prepared by the Anne Frank House in Amsterdam, a museum and foundation committed to promoting world tolerance and peace. Photos from the Anne Frank House archive are supplemented with those from the collections of the woman who helped hide the Frank family and the widow of Anne's father, Otto. Combined with excerpts from Anne's diary and a clear narration, the result is a moving portrait of the idealistic young girl and the times she lived through. An American Library Association Notable Book for 1994.

Wild, Margaret
A Time for Toys
Illustrated by Julie Vivas
Kids Can Press, 1991
Ages 8-12, unpaged
ISBN 1-55074-023-7

Written with haunting simplicity by Margaret Wild and complemented by Julie Vivas' startling and disturbing illustrations, *A Time for Toys* is based on a true incident. In the closing days of World War II, starving women in Bergen-Belsen concentration camp, waiting to be either saved by the advancing British army or massacred by their Nazi jailers, secretly began making toys for the few surviving children. They used scraps of cloth torn from their ragged coats, bits of buttons, and strands of thread to fashion a patchwork doll and a stuffed elephant and owl for the youngest camp prisoners, who had no recollection of playing with toys. While *A Time for Toys* is ultimately a life-affirming story that distils the enormity of the Holocaust to a level that young children can relate to, a book of this impact clearly calls for parents and teachers to exercise discretion.

Korea

Choi, Sook Nyul
Year of Impossible Goodbyes
Dell/Yearling Paperbacks, 1993
Ages 10-15, 169 pp.
ISBN 0-440-40759-1

It is 1945, and the Japanese army is occupying Korea. Ten-year-old Sookan's father is away fighting with the resistance in Manchuria and her mother is forced to supervise a factory producing socks for the Imperial Japanese army. The Korean people are forced to speak Japanese and pray in the Shinto temple of their occupiers. When the war ends, the Koreans rejoice in their freedom. Unfortunately, it does not last long, as Communist troops take control of North Korea, and the people are again subjected to foreign oppression. The suspenseful story of Sookan's family's flight across rice paddies, railroad bridges and towering barbed wire fences to escape to freedom in South Korea will grip adolescent readers.

The sequel, *Echoes of the White Giraffe* (Houghton Mifflin, 1993: ISBN 0-395-64721-5—hardcover; 0440-40970-5—paperback—Dell/Yearling), finds Sookan at 15, coming of age in the South Korean city of Pusan, where she continues to hope that the civil war will end and her family will be reunited in Seoul.

Climo, Shirley
The Korean Cinderella
Illustrated by Ruth Heller
HarperCollins, 1993
Ages 4-8, unpaged
ISBN 0-06-020433-8

This Korean version of the Cinderella tale contains all the familiar elements of the story: Pear Blossom, the beautiful young girl mistreated by her stepmother and stepsister; the lost slipper (in this case, a straw sandal); and the handsome young man who finds the shoe and embarks on a quest to make its owner his bride. In this version, Cinderella's benefactor is a *tokgabi*, a goblin spirit who lives in the bodies of various creatures. It helps Pear Blossom accomplish otherwise insurmountable tasks so that she may attend the village festival. The riotously colorful illustrations and the explanatory notes about the traditional design elements of and sources used to create the drawings make this book an excellent addition to a multicultural folktale collection.

Ginsburg, Mirra
The Chinese Mirror
Illustrated by Margot Zemach
Voyager/HBJ Paperbacks, 1988
Ages 4-7, unpaged
ISBN 0-15-217508-3

In this retelling of a traditional Korean tale, a mirror is brought from China to a town where nobody has ever seen one before. The strange object wreaks amusing havoc within a family as each member sees a different stranger in it. The spare brush illustrations were inspired by an 18-century genre of Korean painting.

Han, Oki S. & Stephanie Plunkett
Sir Whong and the Golden Pig
Illustrated by Oki S. Han
Dial Books for Young Readers, 1993
Ages 4-8, unpaged
ISBN 0-8037-1345-2

A greedy stranger arrives in a peaceful Korean hamlet to ask its wisest and most prosperous citizen, Sir Whong, for a hefty loan of 1,000 *nyung*, ostensibly to buy medicine for his sick mother. As collateral, the stranger offers a shining golden pig, and the goodhearted Sir Whong is persuaded to lend him the money. But when both the priceless pig and the sick mother turn out to be bogus, Sir Whong proves that he won't be outwitted by a cheating stranger. The soft watercolor illustrations of Korean village life, which include scenes of the town well, traditional house interiors, and a wedding ceremony and feast are a special feature of this quiet and lovely book.

Han, Suzanne Crowder
Korean Folk and Fairy Tales
Hollym International, 1991
Ages 10 and up, 256 pp.
ISBN 0-930878-03-5(hardcover)
       0-930878-04-3 (paperback)

Dragons, goblins, monks, tigers, demonic foxes, supernatural spouses and, of course, people with all their human frailties populate this extensive collection of brief Korean tales. The yarns comprise a representative sampling of Korean stories that have been passed down in both the spoken and written traditions. Included are fables, anecdotes, *pourquoi* tales, fairy tales and tales of the strange and supernatural. This collection makes enjoyable pleasure reading and is an excellent source of material for comparing tales from various cultures.

Haskins, Jim
Count Your Way through Korea
Illustrations by Dennis Hockerman
Carolrhoda Books, 1989
Ages 4-8, unpaged
ISBN 0-87614-348-6

This book is one of a series of "Count Your Way" books that introduces young readers to a new country and culture using the numbers one through 10. In this case, the Korean numbers for one through 10 provide the vehicle for young children to learn about various aspects of Korea and its culture, such as basic geography, traditional folk costumes, foods, children's games, and the development of the Korean Hangul alphabet. While some of the number associations are a bit of a stretch, such as nine baseball players on a team showing that baseball is a popular sport in Korea, the overall approach is an appealing way for primary school children to begin exploring another country.

McMahon, Patricia
Chi-Hoon: A Korean Girl
Photographed by Michael F. O'Brien
Boyds Mills Press, 1993
Ages 8-12, 48 pp.
ISBN 1-56397-026-0

This is a photographic diary of a week in the life of eight-year-old Kim Chi-Hoon, who lives with her family in Yoido, a bustling section of the huge city of Seoul. Excerpts in Chi-Hoon's own words are interspersed with clearly written text describing the daily lives of Korean children and their families, at school, home, temple and play. Strong color photographs provide a visual anchor for the narration and a fascinating glimpse into the everyday business of childhood in Korea.

O'Brien, Anne Sibley
The Princess and the Beggar: A Korean Folktale
Scholastic, 1993
Ages 4-8, unpaged
ISBN 0-590-46092-7

In this adaptation of a Korean tale believed to date back to the sixth century, the king's youngest daughter becomes known as the Weeping Princess because she bursts into tears over every little thing. The princess hides from the incessant teasing of the royal court with her books and poetry, until she is banished for refusing to marry the nobleman her father has selected for her. She doesn't want the empty life of running a noble household with only parties and gossip as superficial diversions.

Then, when the princess begins a new life with the poor, filthy beggar, Pabo Ondal, she radically changes both his life and her own. The metamorphosis of the Weeping Princess into the beggar's mentor and champion adds a timely feminist spin to a traditional folktale that will appeal to readers of all ages. The illustrations, which include a recurring motif of traditional Korean seals derived from folk symbols, such as the sun and moon, heaven and earth, and flowers, such as the lotus and plum blossom, provide a rich look at traditional Korean culture.

Rhee, Nami
Magic Spring: A Korean Folktale
Putnam, 1993
Ages 4-8, unpaged
ISBN 0-399-22420-3

Throughout history, people have dreamed of discovering the legendary fountain of youth. In this story, a poor but uncomplaining old Korean couple stumbles upon a spring that can replenish the vigor and strength of their youth, then share the secret with their greedy neighbor. In this tale of just desserts, the effect of the sweet spring water on the neighbor is very different from its effect on the selfless couple. A special touch on each page of this book is an excerpt from the text printed in Korean characters.

The Middle East

Alexander, Sue
Nadia the Willful
Illustrated by Lloyd Bloom
Knopf Paperbacks, 1983
Ages 6-10, unpaged
ISBN 0-679-83480-X

Hamed, a young Bedouin boy, is lost forever in a raging desert sandstorm, bringing boundless grief to his father, Sheik Tarik. After a seven-day period of mourning, Tarik emerges from his tent to command that no one in the clan may ever mention Hamed's name again. "Punishment shall be swift for those who would remind me of what I have lost," he proclaims. But Nadia, Hamed's beloved sister, cannot allow her grief to go unexpressed; for her, never speaking again of Hamed would be a denial of his existence. Nadia defies her father's decree and helps him understand that to speak of Hamed is a not a cruel reminder of his death, but a way of achieving peaceful acceptance of it. This fine story deals with a profound issue in a way that is accessible to children.

Ashabranner, Brent
Gavriel and Jemal: Two Boys of Jerusalem
Photographed by Paul Conklin
Putnam, 1984
Ages 9-12, 95 pp.
ISBN 0-396-08455-9

Though they never meet, Gavriel, an Israeli Jew, and Jemal, a Palestinian Arab, grow up within a kilometer of each other in the Old City of Jerusalem. This book portrays their daily lives, focusing on the many similarities between them. Although the tensions between Israelis and Palestinians are not ignored, the emphasis is on their common experiences. While some information is dated (e.g., references to the ravages of the hyper-inflation of the mid-1980s on the lifestyle of the average Israeli), the book concludes with a message that is still timely: "Other countries and people may help or hinder, but only these two ancient peoples who have their roots in the same ancient land can find a way to lasting peace."

Bider, Djemma
A Drop of Honey
Illustrated by Armen Kojoyian
Simon and Schuster, 1989
Ages 4-8, unpaged
ISBN 0-671-66265-1

Anayida, a young Armenian girl falls asleep and dreams that she is in the market buying the ingredients needed to prepare a tray of sweet, flaky baklava pastries. Pistachios, fragrant cinnamon bark, dried lemon peel and a jar of golden liquid honey are all on her shopping list. But as Anayida buys the honey, a drop spills onto the cobblestones. A bee is attracted by the honey, a cat stalks the bee, and a dog chases the cat. As tables are overturned and pyramids of melons and pomegranates scatter on the ground, the entire market is in an uproar—all because of a single drop of honey. The pastel illustrations do a nice job of conveying the richness of textures and smells in the market. Included at the conclusion of the story is a recipe for baking Armenian baklava.

Dolphin, Laurie
Neve Shalom/Wahat al-Salam: Oasis of Peace
Photographed by Ben Dolphin
Scholastic, 1993
Ages 8-12, 48 pp.
ISBN 0-590-45799-3

This book reduces the complexities of the conflict between Jews and Arabs in Israel/Palestine to terms comprehensible to young readers. The focus is on two 10-year-old boys: Shlomo Franklin, a Jewish Israeli, and Muhammad Jabar, an Arab Israeli. Both are entering a unique school, Neve Shalom/Wahat al-Salam, which is jointly run by Arabs and Jews to foster peaceful co-existence and understanding between the two peoples. Located outside Jerusalem, the progressive school is the first comprehensive Arab-Jewish school in Israel that is both bilingual and bicultural. Initially, the two boys have no common language, but after studying Arabic and Hebrew and learning about each other's cultures, they discover they have much in common and begin to develop a bond of mutual respect and friendship. The photo essay depicts the similarities between the lives of the two boys, showing us their families, homes, friends, leisure activities and love of farm animals.

The book briefly chronicles the development of the school, which has been nominated four times for the Nobel Peace Prize. A page of history about the area and its conflicts is included, up to the first sitting of Jews and Palestinians at peace talks in 1991. There is a short glossary of Arabic and Hebrew words used in the text, as well as an interesting comparison of the Arabic and Hebrew languages, in which the words for things such as olive, night, day, wind and—most important—peace, share a common root.

Edwards, Michelle
Chicken Man
Lothrop, Lee & Shepard, 1991
Ages 4-8, unpaged
ISBN 0-688-09708

On a *kibbutz*, or collective farm, in Israel's Jezreel Valley lives Rody, a good fellow who revels in his job taking care of the chickens. The hens never laid more eggs and the roosters never strutted and crowed more proudly. But Rody's enjoyment of his job works against him: another *kibbutznik* covets his apparently choice position. Thus begins a circular tale of changing work assignments. Every time Rody is given a new chore, his upbeat attitude makes it seem like the choice assignment in the community. Then, one day, the chickens can no longer get along without him and the *kibbutzniks* must set things right. Prefaced with a map picturing the layout of a typical *kibbutz* and followed by a brief appendix describing modern *kibbutz* life, this book introduces young children to both a different way of life and a different perspective on the concept of sharing. Winner of the National Jewish Book Award for children's books.

Grover, Wayne
Ali and the Golden Eagle
Greenwillow Books, 1993
Ages 10-14, 150 pp.
ISBN 0-688-11385-0

Based on author Wayne Grover's experiences working as an engineer in Saudi Arabia during the late 1970s, this is the story of an American man's friendship with

Ali, a 14-year-old boy from Ezratu, a remote village in the Saudi mountains. When Grover captures a baby falcon and gives it to Ali, the boy works long and hard to train the falcon and becomes a master falconer. The relationship between the wild bird and Ali defies understanding, and they are invited by the Saudi royal family to enter a falconry contest. As the Saudi royal family begins to take an interest in the welfare of the inhabitants, the secluded village is suddenly catapulted into the 20th century.

Heide, Florence Parry & Judith Heide Gilliland
Sami and the Time of the Troubles
Illustrated by Ted Lewin
Clarion Books, 1992
Ages 6-12, unpaged
ISBN 0-395-55964-2

Beirut, the capital of Lebanon and locus of the brutal 1975-1990 civil war, is the home of 10-year-old Sami and his family. Sami and his little sister, Leila, are like children everywhere, though they are different in one respect: they have been forced to adjust their lives to the war. For example, during bombardments, they retreat to their uncle's basement, where they dream of what life was like before the fighting began. Ted Lewin's beautiful watercolor illustrations evoke bittersweet moments, such as a wedding that takes place against a backdrop of destroyed buildings, or the children huddling with their mother in the basement on a treasured, richly textured Oriental carpet. Although this book treats the subject of children and war very sensitively, care must be taken when presenting it to refugee children, who may be reluctant to discuss their own, similar experiences.

Heide, Florence Parry & Judith Heide Gilliland
The Day of Ahmed's Secret
Illustrated by Ted Lewin
Lothrop, Lee & Shepard, 1990
Ages 5-10, unpaged
ISBN 0-688-08894-5

Young Ahmed is bursting to share his secret with his family. But before he can do this, he has a full day of work ahead in the bustling city of Cairo. Through ancient gates and crowded alleyways, Ahmed steers his donkey cart loaded with canisters of butane gas for cooking. Against the lush backdrop provided by the watercolor illustrations of the Egyptian city, Ahmed delivers the gas to his customers, taking pride in his ability to lug the heavy bottles by himself. Finally, when his work is finished, he hurries home to share his secret, one that will make his future as a child in the developing world just a bit brighter. The sensitivity and realism of the portrayal of Ahmed's daily life, combined with the universal theme of taking pride in a special accomplishment, make this a multicultural book to treasure.

Hicyilmaz, Gaye
Against the Storm
Puffin Books, 1992
Ages 12 and up, 176 pp.
ISBN 0-14-036073-5

Eleven-year-old Mehmet and his family decide to uproot themselves from their small Turkish village and move to Ankara in search of a better life. But when they arrive in the huge city, their dreams of a flat with running water and electricity evaporate as they must live in a crowded, dirty shanty town, where daily existence seems bleaker than it ever was in the village. In an inspiring show of courage, Mehmet disentangles himself from the precarious life of the shanty town and makes his way back to his village to search for a better life on his home turf.

Hicyilmaz, Gaye
The Frozen Waterfall
Faber & Faber Paperbacks, 1994
Ages 12 and up, 277 pp.
ISBN 0-571-17161-3

The struggle to adjust to life in a rich but confusing society is seen through the eyes of Selda, a 12-year-old Turkish girl who journeys with her mother and sisters to join her guestworking father in Switzerland. Bright and ambitious, Selda is determined to succeed, despite the language barrier, intolerance and lack of funds. A particular strength of this well-written novel is the descriptions of Selda's experiences with a new land and culture, whether it is her first encounter with snow or a trip to buy forbidden blue jeans. Especially powerful are the glimpses into the netherworld of illegal workers, who are trapped between their longing for home and their desire to send poor relatives at home crucial foreign currency.

Kimmel, Eric
The Three Princes: A Tale from the Middle East
Illustrated by Leonard Everett Fisher
Holiday House, 1994
Ages 4-10, unpaged
ISBN 0-8234-1115-X

Once there was a princess who was as wise as she was beautiful. Many sought her hand in marriage, but her preferred suitors were the three princes, Fahad, Muhammed and Mohsen. Of the three, her favorite was Prince Mohsen. Though he was not rich like the others, something drew her to him immediately. Because the kingdom's chief minister thought Mohsen was not wealthy enough for her, the princess decided to put her suitors to a test: she promised to marry the one who brought her the greatest wonder after spending a year roaming the world. When the princess finally makes her choice, she reveals that she is indeed wise. Leonard Everett Fisher's colored chalk drawings softly echo the essence of the Middle Eastern world presented in this story, which exists in the Egyptian, Moroccan and Persian traditions.

Laird, Elizabeth
Kiss the Dust
Mammoth Paperbacks, 1991
Ages 12-16, 279 pp.
ISBN 0-7497-0857-3

Tara is a young Kurdish girl whose family must flee its town for the mountains of Iraqi Kurdistan. The family witnesses Iraqi bombing raids and makes a nighttime trek across the border to Iran, where they are shunted from one refugee camp to another until they finally win political asylum in Britain. Although the tone is upbeat, the book stresses Tara's flexibility and determination in dealing with adversity, providing readers with a rare glimpse of the political and social realities for people in war-torn nations. A good addition to a multicultural reading program in Grades 5-8, this book is also suitable for study by high school ESL classes.

Manson, Christopher
A Gift for the King: A Persian Tale
Henry Holt, 1989
Ages 5-10, unpaged
ISBN 0-8050-0951-5

Based on a tale from the Middle Ages, this is the story of the rich Persian King Artaxerxes, whose subjects show their esteem by lavishing every conceivable luxury on him. On a walk outside the palace grounds one day, the king encounters his army generals, his royal stargazers, a caravan of foreign traders and a group of ambassadors from a neighboring kingdom, all of whom bestow upon him rare and priceless gifts. But it is a poor shepherd boy who gives the most precious gift of all, one that helps the king realize the true meaning of generosity. This tale of a simple gift given from the heart makes a nice counterpoint to *The Stonecutter* (see page 147).

Nye, Naomi Shihab
Sitti's Secrets
Illustrated by Nancy Carpenter
Four Winds Press, 1994
Ages 5-10, unpaged
ISBN 0-02-768460-1

Mona lies in her bed at night and thinks of her grandmother, her *sitti*, who lives in a West Bank Palestinian village halfway around the world. She remembers her trip to Sitti's village and how, although her father had to translate for them, there was much that she and Sitti could share because of their special bond. When Mona returns to the United States, she writes a letter describing Sitti's life to the President. It concludes: "Mr. President, I wish you my good luck in your very hard job. I vote for peace. My grandmother votes with me."

Without engaging in overtly political rhetoric, Naomi Shihab Nye effectively conveys the message that the real meaning of the Middle East conflict lies in the way it touches lives on an intensely personal level. Nancy Carpenter's outstanding illustrations further reinforce this theme. When Mona is in her own bedroom, the moonlit shadows spread a weblike map over her, illuminating the physical distance between her and her grandmother. But when she visits Sitti, Carpenter's artistry underlines human connectedness, as the tattoos on Sitti's hands and the Arabic calligraphy of her greetings gracefully meld into the flight of birds in the blue Middle Eastern sky.

Palacek, Libuse & Josef
The Magic Grove
Picture Book Studio USA, 1985
Ages 6-10, unpaged
ISBN 0-907234-72-0

Two friends, a shepherd and a farmer, cannot decide what to do with a treasure trove of gold they have found buried beneath their land. Finally, they agree to plant a grove of sturdy, beautiful trees for everyone to enjoy. As the shepherd's son travels across the expansive Persian savanna on his way to the city to buy seedlings for the grove, he encounters a strange royal caravan and is faced with a dilemma. Should he continue to the city market as planned, or should he use his gold to free a captive flock of beautiful birds on their way to be slaughtered for the Khan's banquet table? This Persian folktale highlights human values with an imaginative touch of the supernatural and a lyrical use of prose.

Schami, Rafik
A Hand Full of Stars
Translated by Rika Lesser
Dell Paperbacks, 1992
Ages 14 and up, 197 pp.
ISBN 0-440-40892-X

Inspired by his closest friend and mentor, 75-year-old Uncle Salim, a Damascus teenager coming of age in the 1960s resolves to start a journal to record his impressions and feelings about life, school, and his newest girlfriend. At first, the journal is little more than a spirited chronicle of the narrator's existence in a working-class neighborhood. But in response to the political oppression that exists in Syria at the time, it soon becomes a vehicle for the young writer to explore his anger and helplessness at the injustices he witnesses. Finally, taking a courageous stand, he and a group of friends launch an underground newspaper. Although readers come to know the diary's author through his powerful writing, his name is never revealed, an evocative symbol of the refuge provided by anonymity in the face of a repressive political regime.

Stanley, Diane
Fortune
Morrow Junior Books, 1990
Ages 5-10, unpaged
ISBN 0-688-07210-0

Omar, a poor farmer in ancient Persia, does not have enough money to wed his betrothed, the clever Sunny. As result, Sunny sends him to the market town to seek his fortune. But once he arrives at the market, Omar spends all his money on a dancing tiger, which he names Fortune. To Omar's surprise, the dancing tiger brings him great success, so much so that he now feels he has a more lofty destiny than the humble Sunny, and he bids her farewell. On his travels, however, Omar learns some truths about true love and good fortune—and is fortunate that Sunny will still have him when he eventually returns. Reminiscent of delicate Persian miniatures, the illustrations in this book are filled with beautiful mahogany fretwork, graceful calligraphy and shimmering peacocks.

Taylor, Allegra
A Kibbutz in Israel
Photographed by Nancy Durrell McKenna
Lerner Publications, 1987
Ages 6-12, 32 pp.
ISBN 0-8225-1678-0

Tal Niv is 10 years old and lives in Kibbutz Erez, on the edge of Israel's Negev desert. The photographs and text of this well-written book help young readers learn about the communal experience that characterizes life on an Israeli *kibbutz*. We see the children's house where Tal spends his days, the common dining room, the school, athletic facilities and communal store. To avoid giving children the impression that everyone in Israel lives on a *kibbutz*, teachers should be careful to point out that this is not a lifestyle chosen by most people; in fact, *kibbutzim* make up only about three per cent of the country's population. The information in this book nicely complements Michelle Edward's picture book, *Chicken Man* (see page 137). *A Kibbutz in Israel* was published in Britain by A & C Black, under the title, *Tal Niv's Kibbutz*.

South Asia

Axworthy, Anni
Anni's India Diary
Whispering Coyote Press, 1992
Ages 7-10, unpaged
ISBN 1-87085-59-3

Through the eyes of a fictional 10-year-old guide, this book presents an introduction to the land and people of India in a unique diary and scrapbook format. As Anni describes her three-month journey across the Indian subcontinent, colorful illustrations of people and scenery spill over onto photographs, labels, stamps, tickets stubs and other memorabilia, which are the stuff of scrapbooks. The young narrator's chatty, conversational style makes her experiences come alive. This book provides a wonderful inspiration for students to compile a scrapbook of their own travel or immigration experiences.

Barker, Carol
Ananda in Sri Lanka: A Story of Buddhism
Hamish Hamilton, 1985
Ages 8-12, unpaged
ISBN 0-241-11266-4

This author-illustrated information book describes the everyday life of Ananda, a 12-year-old boy living in the small settlement of Turuwila in Sri Lanka. It shows him at home with his family, at school, helping to thresh rice in the fields, and worshipping at the temple. The book also outlines the basic principles of the Buddhist faith and illustrates how Buddhist beliefs permeate the every aspect of the villagers' lives. Although Carol Barker neglects to mention the Tamil minority of Sri Lanka, she does present a rich portrait of the materially poor, yet spiritually rich, existence of Sri Lankan villagers.

Birch, David
The King's Chessboard
Illustrated by Devis Grebu
Dial Books for Young Readers, 1988
Ages 6-12, unpaged
ISBN 0-8037-0365-1

A proud ancient Indian king insists that a wise man who has served him well—and asked nothing in return—choose a reward. The ruler readily grants the wise man's carefully considered request for some grains of rice for each square on the king's chessboard. Too vain to admit his puzzlement, the monarch learns a valuable lesson when he is drawn into the mathematical conundrum created by the wise man's seemingly simple request. This tale has wonderful applications in mathematics and literature programs.

The Rajah's Rice (W.H. Freeman, 1994: ISBN 0-7167-6568-3), by David Barry, is another version of this story. A Scientific American Book for Young Readers, it incorporates a young elephant bather named Chandra, who is entranced by the mathematical world. It is this young girl who presents the numerical conundrum to the king. A helpful note and visual chart about the powers of two round out this book.

Bond, Ruskin
Cherry Tree
Illustrated by Allan Eitzen
Boyds Mills Press, 1991
Ages 4-8, unpaged
ISBN 1-878093-21-5

Six-year-old Rakhi lives in a village in the rocky Himalayan foothills of northern India. After returning from the local bazaar with a trove of sweet, red cherries, Rakhi plants a cherry pit with the guidance of her grandfather. It soon sprouts and, as Rakhi grows older, she and her grandfather watch the tree grow bigger, put forth a profusion of pink blossoms and, finally, give fruit. *Cherry Tree* is a lovely, peaceful and universal story about a little girl experiencing wonder at the changes time can bring.

Gavin, Jamila
The Wheel of Surya
Methuen, 1992
Ages 12-16, 288 pp.
ISBN 0-416-18572-X (hardcover)
        0-7497-1582-0 (paperback—Mammoth)

Caught in the war raging in newly independent India, Marvinder Singh and her younger brother, Jaspal, flee their native Punjab, seeking safety and a new life overseas. Separated from their mother, the pair manage to stow away on a ship bound for England, where Marvinder is reunited with her longtime friend, Edith Chadwick, an English girl who had lived near the Singhs in Punjab. British writer Jamila Gavin's family saga artfully captures the horrors of the Indian war of independence, as well as the difficulties faced by Indian refugee families in post-war Britain.

Hodges, Margaret
The Golden Deer
Illustrated by Daniel Dan Souci
Scribners, 1992
Ages 5-8, unpaged
ISBN 0-684-19218-7

From the centuries-old Indian classic, *The Jakata: Stories of the Buddha's Former Births*, comes this tale of the reincarnation of the Buddha in the form of a golden deer in the holy Indian city of Benares. The enchanted deer protects his herd from the king's hunters, thus bringing about the freedom of all living creatures on earth.

Jaffrey, Madhur
Seasons of Splendour: Tales, Myths and Legends of India
Puffin Paperbacks, 1992
Ages 10 and up, 186 pp.
ISBN 0-14-034699-6

Well-known Indian cookbook author Madhur Jaffrey turns her talents to recounting some of India's rich legends and folklore. Readers can follow the life of the great god Krishna, find out how monkey god Hanuman helped defeat the Demon King Ravan, and learn how the god Ganesh got his elephant head. The stories are arranged according to the sequence of the Hindu calendar, and there are short anecdotes about the festivals that have grown around the folktales.

Mathieson, Feroza
The Very Special Sari
Photographs by Prodeepta Das
A & C Black, 1988
Ages 3-8, 25 pp.
ISBN 0-7136-3064-7

Because Gita's mother has a very special wedding to attend, she decides to have an elegant new sari tailored for the occasion. Together, Gita and her mother select the opulent silk and the beads and sequins to decorate it, and deliver the materials to Mrs. Nayak, the dressmaker. Thoroughly dazzled by the finery being prepared for her mother, Gita, too, dreams of a new outfit and, by story's end, she is not disappointed. This book is one of a series published by A & C Black that is designed to reflect the experiences of young children in various countries through simple text and color photographs. Other titles include *The Very Hot Samosas* (Pakistan); *The Perfect Present* (Barbados); and *Whatever Next?* (Trinidad).

Newton, Pam
The Stonecutter
Putnam, 1990
Ages 5-10, unpaged
ISBN 0-399-22187-5

A modest stonecutter in ancient India is happy with his lot in life until he enters the luxurious residence of a wealthy merchant. From then on, the stonecutter prays that he may one day have riches himself. In time, the spirits within the mountain where he spends his days chiseling and polishing decide to grant his wish. But when he achieves his desire, his covetousness does not cease—and so begins a circular tale of dissatisfaction and longing that ends only when the stonecutter is finally transformed back into his original humble—and contented—self. Lavish illustrations in a style reminiscent of ancient Indian art complete this lovely picture book.

Rodanas, Kristina
The Story of Wali Dad
Lothrop, Lee & Shepard, 1988
Ages 6-10, unpaged
ISBN 0-688-07262-3

Wali Dad is an old Indian fieldworker who lives a simple life and is truly satisfied with his meager possessions. When he finally saves enough money to buy something substantial, Wali Dad finds he has no need of luxuries for himself; instead, he buys a beautiful bracelet to send to the Princess of Khaistan, whom he has heard is the kindest and most beautiful woman in the area. This simple act of generosity sparks a chain of events in which Wali Dad finds himself playing matchmaker between the princess and a neighboring prince. This gently charming tale is beautifully illustrated in jewel-toned colors.

Rose, Deborah Lee
The People Who Hugged the Trees
Illustrated by Birgitta Saflund
Roberts Rinehart, 1992
Ages 6-10, unpaged
ISBN 0-91197-80-7 (hardcover)
    1-879373-50-5 (paperback)

In this tale, which originated in 17th-century Rajasthan, the villagers in a hamlet protected from the ravages of desert storms by a lush grove of trees stage a "sit-in" to prevent the maharajah's men from cutting the trees to supply wood for his palace. Delicate watercolor illustrations provide a soft backdrop for the story. This tale provides an excellent opportunity to demonstrate that people from all cultures are interested in protecting our natural environment.

Roth, Susan L.
Buddha
Doubleday, 1994
Ages 5-10, unpaged
ISBN 0-385-31072-2

Enhanced by imaginative paper-collage illustrations, this is the story of the early years of Prince Siddhartha, who would one day become Buddha, the Enlightened One, to followers around the world. To circumvent a prophecy that his son would grow to be a very holy man, King Shuddhodana raises Siddhartha in splendid isolation in the royal compound, free of all cares and concerns. But when, as an adult, Siddhartha finally ventures beyond the palace gates and sees the misery around him, he begins the long spiritual journey that fulfils the prophecy. Particularly effective is the juxtaposition of the descriptions of Siddhartha's blissful existence in the palace with the scenes of sickness, agony and death that he witnesses outside its walls.

Shepard, Aaron
Savitri: A Tale of Ancient India
Illustrated by Vera Rosenberry
Albert Whitman, 1992
Ages 6-10, unpaged
ISBN 0-8075-7251-9

The well-known tale of Princess Savitri appears in the *Mahabharata*, an epic Hindu religious text. Strong-willed Savitri chooses to marry Satyavan, knowing that he is doomed to die within a year. Through her quick-wittedness, however, she succeeds in winning his soul back from the grasp of Yama, the God of Death. A portrait of an independent and wise woman, the text combines with the illustrations to create an authentic, if stylized, vision of classical India.

Staples, Suzanne Fisher
Shabanu: Daughter of the Wind
Knopf, 1989
Ages 12 and up, 256 pp.
ISBN 0-394-94815-7 (hardcover)
     0-679-81030-7 (paperback—Knopf/Borzoi)

Life is both satisfying and brutal for strong-willed, 12-year-old Shabanu, the younger daughter in a family of modern-day Pakistani camel herders. Shabanu loves the freedom of her nomadic life in the windswept Cholistan Desert of Pakistan, and her role in caring for the family's camel herd. She and her 13-year-old sister, Phulan, are betrothed to brothers who are considered good matches because they own land in the irrigated area of the desert. Shabanu accepts this arranged marriage as her duty to her family, although she is apprehensive about the life that will be in store for her. But a calamitous encounter with a wealthy and powerful landowner changes her future forever. To smooth over a feud, she is promised to the landowner's brother as his fourth wife. Shabanu meets her destiny with the knowledge that there will always be a part of her that she can keep free from the demands of the strictly defined role her new situation demands. A Newbery Honor Book in 1990.

Staples, Suzanne Fisher
Haveli
Knopf, 1993
Ages 12 and up, 264 pp.
ISBN 0-679-84157-1

In this powerful sequel to *Shabanu* (see previous entry), five years have passed and Shabanu has fulfilled her duty by becoming the fourth wife of the prosperous Rahim. With her young daughter, Mumtaz, she lives in his *haveli* (a traditional three-story urban house owned by prestigious Pakistani families) in Lahore, where she must deal with the malice of his three senior wives. Then, Shabanu falls unexpectedly in love with Rahim's nephew, Omar, a forbidden liaison that could be punishable by death at the hands of her husband. Once again, the independent-minded Shabanu is trapped by the centuries-old traditions of her culture that make fulfilling her dreams impossible. These two books are noteworthy both for their engrossing, suspenseful plots and their insightful portrayal of a young woman caught in the tug-of-war between tradition and independence.

Tagore, Rabindranath
Paper Boats
Illustrated by Grace Bochak
Boyds Mills Press, 1992
Ages 4-8, 32 pp.
ISBN 1-878093-12-6

Rabindranath Tagore, born in Calcutta in 1861, was an essayist, poet and playwright who won the Nobel Prize for Literature in 1913. His brief but lyrical poem, "Paper Boats," in which a young Indian boy sends small boats crafted from paper down the river to strange and unknown lands, is brought to life by equally simple folded paper illustrations portraying the rural world of the young builder of the boats.

Southeast Asia

Boholm-Olsson, Eva
Tuan
Illustrated by Pham van Don
Farrar, Straus & Giroux, 1988
Ages 5-8, unpaged
ISBN 91-29-58766-2

Translated from the original Swedish, this picture book tells the story of Tuan, a little boy growing up in contemporary rural Vietnam. When Tuan is bitten by a rabid dog, his mother rushes him to a clinic in the city, only to discover that the doctor may not be able to obtain the vaccine needed to save her son's life. In the end, the situation is resolved positively, but the book accurately describes the day-to-day realities of life for a child in the developing world. *Tuan* is illustrated with luminous silk paintings done by Pham van Don, an artist at the Hanoi Academy of Art.

Carrison, Muriel Paskin
Cambodian Folk Stories from the Gatiloke
Charles E. Tuttle, 1993
Ages 10-adult, 139 pp.
ISBN 0-8048-1905-X

The Gatiloke is a collection of ancient Cambodian folk stories that were handed down orally for many hundreds of years, and committed to paper only in the late 19th century. Originating in the teachings of Cambodian Buddhist monks, the stories of the Gatiloke—which means roughly "the right way for the people of the world to live"—illustrate Buddhist precepts about human relations, greed, punishment and reward, and reverence for animals. Accompanied by an extensive section of notes on Cambodian history and culture, a glossary, maps and a supplementary reading list, this anthology is an excellent introduction to the literary tradition of the Cambodian people.

Garland, Sherry
Song of the Buffalo Boy
Harcourt Brace, 1992
Ages 12 and up, 282 pp.
ISBN 0-15-277107-7 (hardcover)
     0-15-200098-4 (paperback)

When the United States military withdrew from Vietnam in 1975, many American soldiers left children behind—"Amerasians" like 17-year-old Loi, whose fellow villagers ostracize her because she is *con-lai*, a half-breed, and a reminder of their country's tragic civil war. Only Khai, a young buffalo herder, shows Loi love and understanding. Loi and Khai secretly pledge to marry, but their plans are rudely shattered when Loi is promised in marriage to a Vietnamese army officer. Loi flees to Ho Chi Minh City. When Loi gets the opportunity to emigrate to the United States under the Amerasian Homecoming Program, she must decide whether she will abandon everything she has ever known for the totally unknown. Although the ending is syrupy, this book does a creditable job of realistically depicting life in rural and urban postwar Vietnam.

Ho, Minfong
The Clay Marble
Farrar, Straus & Giroux Paperbacks, 1991
Ages 12-16, 163 pp.
ISBN 0-374-41229-4

A moving novel drawn from the author's experiences as a worker in the refugee camps, this is the story of the flight of 12-year-old Dara and her family from the killing fields of Cambodia. The family establishes a temporary home at a refugee camp on the Thai-Cambodian border, where Dara and her new friend, Jantu, forge an enduring bond of friendship in the makeshift squalor of the camp. But when the inescapable fighting reaches even their place of refuge, Dara is separated from both friend and family and must summon all her courage to find her way back to the people she loves.

Ho, Minfong
Rice without Rain
Lothrop, Lee & Shepard, 1990
Ages 12 and up, 36 pp.
ISBN 0-688-06355-1

A searing drought has brought appalling hardship to 17-year-old Jinda's farming village of Maekung in Thailand. When a group of social rebels from Bangkok University comes to the rural village to promote political resistance, Jinda falls in love with Ned, the leader. Learning from Ned ideas of revolutionary reform that split the villagers into two opposing camps, Jinda comes to realize that political change must take place if her family's beloved rural existence is to continue.

Huynh, Quang Nhuong
The Land I Lost: Adventures of a Boy in Vietnam
Illustrated by Vo-Dinh Mai
HarperTrophy Paperbacks, 1986
Ages 8-12, 129 pp.
ISBN 0-06-440183-9

In these action-packed reminiscences of his youth in a small village in the central highlands of Vietnam, author Huynh Quang Nhuong recounts his boyhood encounters with pythons, wild hogs, crocodiles and monkeys. He paints a vivid picture of life in his rural hamlet, where the villagers live in bamboo houses covered with coconut leaves and the children look forward to the day when they will be old enough to accompany their fathers to the jungle to hunt. A continuing theme in the book is the narrator's relationship with his beloved companion, Tank, the water buffalo. An American Library Association Notable Children's Book.

Keller, Holly
Grandfather's Dream
Greenwillow Books, 1994
Ages 5-10, unpaged
ISBN 0-688-12339-2

In 1992, children's author and illustrator Holly Keller joined a group of American and Vietnamese scientists on a working tour of the Mekong Delta. The aim of the international collaboration was to preserve the indigenous Sarus crane, the largest flying bird in the world, whose existence has been threatened since the end of the Vietnam War. Accompanied by soft watercolor illustrations and in a tone devoid of moralizing, the story tells of the successful efforts of one Vietnam village to dam up the floodlands of the Mekong Delta in order to encourage the beautiful birds to return to roost in their original habitat. *Grandfather's Dream* is an excellent multicultural addition to an environmental studies unit in the primary and junior grades.

Lee, Jeanne M.
Ba-Nam
Henry Holt, 1987
Ages 5-8, unpaged
ISBN 0-8050-0169-7

Based on the author's childhood experiences in Vietnam, this is the story of Nan, a young girl who is allowed for the first time to accompany her family on their annual pilgrimage to the graveyard to bestow offerings on their ancestors. Ba-Nam is the wizened, fearsome-looking woman who tends graves at the cemetery. Against a backdrop of shadowy bamboo groves and shrieking monkeys and bats, the old gravekeeper helps Nan come to understand that outward appearances can be deceiving.

Meeker, Clare Hodgson
A Tale of Two Rice Birds
Illustrated by Christine Lamb
Sasquatch Books, 1994
Ages 8 and up, unpaged
ISBN 1-57061-008-8

Imbued with the spirit of the Buddhist faith, *A Tale of Two Rice Birds* retells a beautiful Thai story of lost love regained in another incarnation. Tragedy befalls a pair of rice birds living in the serenity of the rolling rice fields. When their nest is struck by a spark and bursts into flames, the male bird becomes entangled in a plant and is unable to rescue their young. Throwing herself on the ashes to move on to the next life, the grief-stricken female vows never to trust or speak to a male again. Before immolating himself, the male rice bird pledges to win back her love. Reborn as a farmer and a princess, the two slowly rediscover trust and mutual support. The themes of spirituality, reincarnation and enduring devotion make this a picture book that can also be used effectively with both secondary school and adult learners.

Shalant, Phyllis
Look What We've Brought You from Vietnam
Julian Messner, 1988
Ages 6-12, 48 pp.
ISBN 0-671-65978-2 (paperback)

A compendium of crafts, games, recipes, stories and other pastimes from Vietnamese children's culture, this book is packed with activities that will enrich students' multicultural experience. It includes instructions for *O-Lang*, a counting game, recipes for traditional Vietnamese holiday dishes, craft projects such as constructing a New Year's lantern and a "kitchen" kite, and traceable figures and a script for mounting a traditional Vietnamese water puppet play.

Vuong, Lynette Dyer
Sky Legends of Vietnam
Illustrated by Vo-Dinh Mai
HarperCollins, 1993
Ages 10 and up, 103 pp.
ISBN 0-06-023001-0

This collection of old Vietnamese tales and legends contains six stories mined from Lynette Dyer Vuong's study of the world of ancient Vietnamese folklore. The tales revolve around celestial themes, from a *pourquoi* tale explaining why the rooster crows at dawn to the enchanted story of the moon fairy.

In another collection by the same author, *The Golden Carp and Other Tales from Vietnam* (Lothrop, Lee & Shepard, 1993: ISBN 0-688-12514-X), the six yarns revolve around a romance theme, a central motif in Vietnamese lore. Both volumes contain author's notes setting out the background of each story, as well as a pronunciation guide to Vietnamese names. Both these books are good additions to a comparative folklore program.

Vuong, Lynette Dyer
The Brocaded Slipper and Other Vietnamese Tales
HarperTrophy Paperbacks, 1992
Ages 8-12, 111 pp.
ISBN 0-06-440440-4

In this collection of five stories, Lynette Dyer Vuong draws parallels between the Vietnamese fairy tales she presents and such western standards as *Thumbelina, The Frog Prince, Rip van Winkle, Cinderella* and *The Goose Girl*. She presents some interesting perspectives for a comparative study of these Vietnamese tales, enabling students to perceive their unique cultural flavor while appreciating the themes that tie them to their Western counterparts. There is a useful section of author's notes with asides on Vietnamese geography, history and traditions and a clearly explained pronunciation guide.

Wall, Lina Mao & Cathy Spagnoli
Judge Rabbit and the Tree Spirit: A Folktale from Cambodia
Illustrated by Nancy Hom
Children's Book Press, 1991
Ages 4-8, 32 pp.
ISBN 0-89239-071-9

When the troublesome spirit of the banyan tree poses as a young woman's husband who has gone off to war, Judge Rabbit, a lovable and compassionate Cambodian folk hero, takes on the case. With Solomonic wisdom, he devises a foolproof scheme for revealing the identity of the real spouse. This bilingual book in English and Khmer is colorfully illustrated with silkscreen and watercolor paintings.

Xiong, Blia
Nine-in-One, Grr! Grr!
Adapted by Cathy Spagnoli
Illustrated by Nancy Hom
Children's Book Press, 1989
Ages 4-8, 32 pp.
ISBN 0-89239-048-4

A folktale from the Hmong of Laos, this is the story of the great god Shao who promises the tiger that she will give birth to nine tiger cubs every year. Galvanized into action by the thought of the land being overrun by hordes of tigers, Bird comes up with a clever plan to make sure that the tiger will bear far fewer children. The patterned refrain of Shao's incantation will especially appeal to young listeners in read-aloud time. Because the language of the Hmong is only oral, they record their stories on storycloths, a form of wall-hanging that chronicles an event through colorful embroidered scenes. Nancy Hom's illustrations are based on this authentic form of narrative stitchery. An American Library Association Notable Children's Book.

Various Cultures in a Single Book

Anno, Mitsumasa
All in a Day
Illustrated by Raymond Briggs, Ron Brooks, Eric Carle, Gian Calvi, Zhu Chengliand, Leo and Diane Dillon, Akiko Hayashi and Nicolai Ye Popov
Philomel Books, 1986/1992
Ages 7-11, unpaged
ISBN 0-399-61292-0

Like *Nine O'Clock Lullaby* (see page 167), *All in a Day* illustrates the things that unite humankind across the time zones. Ten of the world's best children's illustrators have contributed to showing how children all over the world participate in similar activities during a 24-hour day. Every time a page is turned, three hours have elapsed as we see children's lives in the United States, England, Russia, Japan, Brazil, Kenya, China and Australia. This book includes the author's detailed notes about concepts such as the world's time zones, Greenwich mean time, the international date line and other world time trivia.

De Zutter, Hank
Who Says a Dog Goes Bow-Wow?
Illustrated by Suse Macdonald
Doubleday, 1993
Ages 4-10, unpaged
ISBN 0-385-30659-8

Hank De Zutter's international menagerie—crowing roosters, chattering monkeys, singing birds and grunting pigs—is a wonderful way to introduce the concept that the sounds animals make are represented differently in various languages. Children will notice that some words for animal sounds are very similar, while others are quite different. A wide variety of tongues is represented; from Chinese to Thai, Finnish to Serbo-Croatian, and Lithuanian to Turkish. The text contains one incorrect reference when the language "Ethiopian" is mentioned several times; in fact, the main language of Ethiopia is Amharic. But, no matter, this book is great fun, providing many opportunities for children to share words from their home languages and to crow and cackle in a chorus of animal sounds.

Another notable book in the same genre is Marc Robinson's and Steve Jenkins' *Cock-A-Doodle-Doo! What Does It Sound Like to You?* (Stewart, Tabori & Chang, 1994: ISBN 1-55670-267-1), which expands on the theme by comparing the representation in various languages of water dripping, a train whistling and a hammer banging.

Dooley, Norah
Everybody Cooks Rice
Illustrated by Peter J. Thornton
Scholastic, 1991
Ages 4-9, unpaged
ISBN 0-590-45597-4

When Carrie searches the neighborhood for her younger brother, Anthony, she pops into the neighbors' kitchens as they are preparing dinner and discovers that everybody cooks rice. The Diazes are having yellow rice with pigeon peas, the Krishnamurthy's are cooking biryani stew and basmati rice and the Bleu family from Haiti is enjoying creole-style rice with spicy beans. All the recipes are included with easy-to-follow directions.

Dorros, Arthur
This Is My House
Scholastic, 1992
Ages 4-8, unpaged
ISBN 0-590-45302-5

The text and illustrations of this book depict the various kinds of houses lived in by children all over the world. The words, "This is my house," appear on each page in the appropriate native language and script with an English transliteration. Seventeen different countries are represented, including Bolivia, Hong Kong, Mali, Turkey, New Guinea and Thailand. This book is an excellent complement to *Houses and Homes* (see page 164).

Fisher, Leonard Everett
Alphabet Art: Thirteen ABCs from around the World
Four Winds Press, 1978
Ages 8 and up, 64 pp.
ISBN 0-02-735230-7

This book contains a history and beautiful reproductions of 13 alphabetical systems in use around the world: Arabic, Cherokee, Chinese, Cyrillic, Gaelic, German, Greek, Inuit, Hebrew, Japanese, Sanskrit, Thai and Tibetan. The diverse writing systems display a diversity of directionality and a wonderful variety of visual forms: arcs, angles, flowing lines and rectangular corners. This is an invaluable resource for calligraphy and dual language activities across a variety of cultures and language groups.

Giblin, James Cross
From Hand to Mouth: Or How We Invented Knives, Forks, Spoons, and Chopsticks and the Table Manners to Go with Them
Thomas Y. Crowell, 1987
Ages 8-14, 86 pp.
ISBN 0-690-04660-X

An international, historical survey of the development of eating customs, *From Hand to Mouth* chronicles the evolution of eating utensils around the world, from the earliest archaeological discoveries to modern times. Breezily written and illustrated with photographs of ancient implements and drawings of people at tables the world over, this book provides children with a wonderful introduction to the cultural relativity of eating customs and table manners, from which they can then make the leap to less tangible customs and beliefs.

Hamanaka, Sheila
All the Colors of the Earth
Morrow Junior Books, 1994
Ages 4-8, unpaged
ISBN 0-688-11131-9

This brief but beautiful prose poem celebrates the diversity of children in our world. Soft metaphors describing the wonderful variety of skin colors of the earth's children swirl around lush illustrations that reflect the mosaic of the world's peoples. The laughing, joyful faces and poses of the children add a sense of wonder and excitement to the discovery that, while we may appear different on the outside, we all gain happiness from loving and being loved.

Hoberman, Mary Ann (Ed.)
My Song Is Beautiful: Poems and Pictures in Many Voices
Little, Brown, 1994
Ages 5-12, 32 pp.
ISBN 0-316-36738-9

This collection of poetry includes a number of short selections that focus on the uniqueness of every child, as well as the links that draw all children together. Each of the 14 poems by celebrated authors is illustrated with a painting or photograph in a style as distinct as the culture it represents. Notes are included on all the contributors and their cultural backgrounds. Writers include West Indian storyteller Ashley Bryan, Korean poet Kim Soo-Jang and American children's poet Jack Prelutsky. Also featured is the first poem published by Nicole Hernandez, a seventh grade student from Brooklyn, New York.

Jaffe, Nina
Patakin: World Tales of Drums and Drummers
Illustrated by Ellen Eagle
Henry Holt, 1994
Ages 10-16, 144 pp.
ISBN 0-8050-3005-0

Storyteller and educator Nina Jaffe has compiled a collection of diverse tales with a common theme—the beating of drums, which she describes as one of the most ancient and sacred musical rites. Percussion instruments like the *changgo* of Korea, the Gaelic *bodhran*, and the *lali* of Fiji provide a rhythmic backdrop to these stories and legends that celebrate the world's musical diversity. Most of the stories are accompanied by short musical passages so that readers can try out different rhythms. *Patakin*—a Cuban word of African origin meaning "legend"—also includes a wealth of information on the building of drums and their uses in various cultures.

Jennss, Aylette
Come Home with Me: A Multicultural Treasure Hunt
The New Press, 1993
Ages 8-12, 48 pp.
ISBN 1-56584-064-X

This colorful, upbeat volume was produced in conjunction with "The Kids Bridge," a major exhibit about ethnicity and racism that is touring children's museums across the United States until 1999. In it, readers interactively follow four children through Boston's many different neighborhoods on a treasure hunt for various ethnic services and specialties.

Kherdian, David
Feathers and Tails: Animal Fables from around the World
Illustrated by Nonny Hogrogian
Philomel Books, 1992
Ages 4-10, 96 pp.
ISBN 0-399-21876-9

A rich anthology of animal fables and folktales from sources such as the ancient Roman moralist Aesop, the Middle Eastern Kalila wa Dimna tales, 16th-century Chinese author Wu Cheng-en, African Anansi lore, and the Brothers Grimm from Germany, this book makes an excellent read-aloud for younger listeners. Older readers, on the other hand, will enjoy dipping into the collection for themselves.

Knight, Margy Burns
Talking Walls
Illustrated by Anne Sibley O'Brien
Tilbury House, 1992
Ages 8 and up, unpaged
ISBN 0-88448-102-6

A unique departure in children's literature, *Talking Walls* presents historic, religious and political sites spanning the globe to demonstrate how we can learn about the heritage and history of the world's peoples through their cultural monuments. Some of these monuments were built to divide or imprison people, while others were built to unify a culture. Regardless of its intent, each wall has much to tell us about the values and customs of the society that built it. This book is up-to-date and includes a section on the 1989 fall of the Berlin Wall, as well as the 1990 release from prison of Nelson Mandela, which heralded the crumbling of the wall of *apartheid* that divided the peoples of South Africa.

Available as a companion to *Talking Walls* is a teacher's activity guide containing chapters designed to help develop the study of each culture represented in the book. Suggested activities run the gamut from research projects, invited speakers and field trips, creative writing and literature explorations to cooking and food experiences. An extensive list of print and audio-visual resources accompanies each chapter.

Author and illustrator also collaborated on *Welcoming Babies* (Tilbury House, 1994: ISBN 0-88448-123-9). A celebration of multicultural diversity for the younger set, *Welcoming Babies* presents the traditions and ceremonies for greeting new infants in cultures all over the world. Scaled down in size for tiny hands, the book includes informative notes for early childhood educators wishing to expand on the book's theme.

Lankford, Mary D.
Hopscotch around the World
Illustrated by Karen Milone
Morrow Junior Books, 1992
Ages 6-12, 48 pp.
ISBN 0-688-08419-2

Hopscotch is played all over the world. Although Bolivian children call it *la thunkuna* and Trinidadian kids name it *jumby*, the basic principles are the same no matter where it's played: draw a pattern on the ground or pavement, throw in a stone or marker, and hop or jump your way through without making any mistakes. This collection of 19 versions of the game acknowledges hopscotch as a traditional game that unifies children across cultures. From El Salvador to Germany, and from Italy to Nigeria, the rules and patterns are presented with easy-to-follow instructions so that children can try out variations. As a result of the fast pace of political developments in the world, several countries included in the collection no longer exist. The rich bibliography of sources that Lankford drew on in compiling the collection is a useful guide for conducting research into other childhood games common to many cultures.

Meyer, Carolyn
Rio Grande Stories
Gulliver/Harcourt Brace, 1994
Ages 10-14, 257 pp.
ISBN 0-15-200066-6

The seventh grade students at Albuquerque's Rio Grande Middle School have arrived from feeder schools all over the city. Facing new academic and social challenges, the students are part of a special program known as the Heritage Project, a cross-curricular initiative designed to increase their awareness of their own family history and culture and how these fit into the larger American scene. When asked to embark on a fundraising project for the school, the students decide to write and market their own book. They all contribute something from their cultural background that is important to them. Filled with stories, traditions and recipes, the book becomes a huge success, while the students learn much about themselves and each other. The chapters of *Rio Grande Stories* alternate stories about the students with their contributions to the book, showing how their cultures are linked by the community that is home to them all.

Morris, Ann
Houses and Homes
Photographed by Ken Heyman
Lothrop, Lee & Shepard, 1992
Ages 5-10, 32 pp.
ISBN 0-688-10168-2

An excellent complement to *This Is My House* (see page 159), *Houses and Homes* is a photographic look at houses around the world that have much in common, though their facades may appear very different. The team of writer Ann Morris and photographer Ken Heyman have also collaborated on four other photographic surveys of various aspects of culture around the world: *Bread, Bread, Bread*; *Hats, Hats, Hats*; *Loving*; and *On the Go*. All are available from Lothrop, Lee & Shepard.

Nikola-Lisa, W.
Bein' with You This Way
Illustrated by Michael Bryant
Lee and Low Books, 1994
Ages 4-8, unpaged
ISBN 1-880000-05-9

A delightful book that highlights the joyful commonalities among people, *Bein' with You This Way* is an infectious playground rap led by a young girl whose beaded braids flip as she swings, slides and leapfrogs through the part. Pairs of contrasting adjectives, such as "light" and "dark," "straight" and "curly," and "thick" and "thin," are presented to a snappy rap beat, adding a new twist to a traditional concept.

Nye, Naomi Shihab
This Same Sky: A Collection of Poems from around the World
Four Winds Press, 1992
Ages 8 and up, 212 pp.
ISBN 0-02-768440-7

Naomi Shihab Nye is a poet-in-the-schools whose work has appeared in a number of collections. For this volume, Nye has turned anthologist, collecting 129 works of poetry, many translated from the original language. Representing 68 different countries, the poems are arranged by theme areas such as "Families," "The Earth and Sky in Which We Live," and "Human Mysteries." Uniting all these diverse rhythms is the sense that what we all share is far greater and more important than the differences among us. "You have a long road to travel before you, and tying your shoe is only the first tying," says the Irish poet Maire Mhac an tSaoi in the poem, "The First Shoe." This sentiment shows how we are all joined to one another in our journey through life. This beautifully produced volume includes biographical notes on all the contributors, and comes complete with an attached page-marking ribbon, as any volume of poetry should. The signatures of many of the poets whose work appears in the book are reproduced on the endpapers, along with a selection of the envelopes and stamps that brought their poetry to Nye's desk in the United States.

Osborne, Mary Pope
Mermaid Tales from around the World
Illustrated by Troy Howell
Scholastic, 1993
Ages 8-12, 84 pp.
ISBN 0-590-44377-1

A collection of 12 mermaid tales from around the world, this book features magical creatures from cultures as diverse as North America's First Peoples, Ukraine, Niger, Iran, China and Greece, as well as Hans Christian Andersen's famous enchanted sea maiden.

Parry, Caroline
Let's Celebrate! Canada's Special Days
Kids Can Press, 1987
Ages 8 and up, 256 pp.
ISBN 0-921103-40-9

Canadians from every background and heritage celebrate hundreds of special days throughout the year, whether they are religious or ethnic holidays, birthdays of important heroes or anniversaries of special events. Using the flow of the seasons as a framework, Caroline Parry tells readers about more than 250 days of special significance to a diverse range of Canadians. From the Iroquois Midwinter Festival before the January full moon, to jumping over bonfires at the Iranian Now Ruz festival at the end of March; from Tisha b'Av in midsummer, when Jews fast to mourn the destruction of the Temple in Jerusalem to the autumn Hindu festival of lights known as Diwali; it's all here in catchily written text that includes art, craft and cooking ideas, as well as facts and trivia.

Rattigan, Jama Kim
Dumpling Soup
Illustrated by Lillian Hsu-Flanders
Little, Brown, 1993
Ages 5-9, unpaged
ISBN 0-316-73445-4

Set in Hawaii, *Dumpling Soup* relates how one large Asian-American family with members hailing from a variety of backgrounds celebrates New Year's Day. Because eating first thing on New Year's means that one won't go hungry for the rest of the year, it is a family tradition to start the New Year with steaming bowls of dumpling soup. This year, seven-year-old Marisa is old enough to try making the delectable treats herself. Although her first efforts appear forlorn and lumpy among the other trays of beautifully wrapped dumplings, they are a taste success with everyone. A rollicking mix of languages and customs from Hawaiian, Korean, Japanese and Chinese traditions, this story will encourage youngsters to think about the cultural influences in their own lives.

Rosen, Michael (Ed.)
South and North, East and West: The Oxfam Book of Children's Stories
Candlewick Press, 1992
Ages 6-12, 96 pp.
ISBN 1-56402-117-3

Each story in this collection of 25 traditional tales from countries around the world is illustrated in a distinct style by a different artist. With an introduction by actor-comedian Whoopi Goldberg, the book was produced to coincide with Oxfam's 50th anniversary. All proceeds go to support this organization's projects.

Singer, Marilyn
Nine O'Clock Lullaby
Illustrated by Frané Lessac
HarperTrophy, 1992
Ages 4-8, unpaged
ISBN 0-06-443319-6 (paperback)

While a mother reads a 9 p.m. bedtime story to a child in New York, a girl sneaks a nighttime snack in her pantry in England at 2 a.m., a cat knocks over a samovar in Moscow at 5 a.m., children in India fill buckets of water at 7:30 a.m., a family goes for an afternoon swim in Samoa at 3 p.m., and children say goodnight to their burros in Mexico at 8 p.m. This simple story works both as an introduction to the concept of time zones, as well as to the ties of life experience that bind people around the world.

Terzian, Alexandra M.
The Kids' Multicultural Art Book: Art and Craft Experiences from around the World
Williamson Publishing, 1993
Ages 3-10, 160 pp.
ISBN 0-913589-72-1

This book includes background information and instructions for more than 100 craft projects from African, Native American, Asian and Hispanic cultures. Everything from masks to jewelry, and textile stamping to doll-making can be found in this useful compendium. Winner of a 1993 Parents' Choice Award, this book is a useful complement to the hands-on expansion of themes raised by multicultural children's literature.

Torres, Leyla
Subway Sparrow
Farrar, Straus & Giroux, 1993
Ages 3-8, unpaged
ISBN 0-374-37285-3

A sparrow flies into a subway car on Brooklyn's D train, and the doors slam shut. There are four people in the car, but only two speak English. The others are a Polish-speaking woman and an older Spanish-speaking man. In a chorus of different languages, they work together to coax the little bird closer so they can catch him before the train pulls into the next station, where a large crowd of people is waiting to board. This simple book is a lovely depiction of diverse North American urbanites uniting in a modest common purpose.

Western Europe

Aliki
The Eggs: A Greek Folktale
HarperTrophy Paperbacks, 1994
Ages 4-8, unpaged
ISBN 0-06-443385-4

A sea captain is dining on four fried eggs at an inn near the harbor when a storm blows up. He dashes away to save his precious boat, forgetting to pay the owner for the food. Six years later, the mariner drops anchor at the same port and immediately heads for the inn to make good his debt. But the innkeeper demands 500 gold pieces for the eggs, the amount he declares would be his if he had been able to hatch the four eggs and start a prosperous chicken farm. With the help of a canny lawyer, the sailor navigates around the innkeeper's outrageous charges and returns, still solvent, to his beloved sea. This engaging retelling of an old Greek tale will interest teachers of older learners as it can spark discussion of tales with similar themes of foiling trickery.

Another equally charming Greek folktale retold by Aliki is *Three Gold Pieces* (HarperTrophy Paperbacks, 1994: ISBN 0-06-443386-2).

Allen, Linda
The Mouse Bride
Philomel Books, 1992
Ages 4-8, unpaged
ISBN 0-399-22136-0

The Mouse Bride is a retelling of an old Finnish tale in which Pekka, the woodsman, follows the instructions of a wise old witch and sends each of his three grown sons into the forest to follow the direction of a felled tree in order to find a bride. The two older sons quickly find suitable mates, but the youngest, Jukka, comes upon a mouse. Disappointed, but wanting to honor his vow to his father, Jukka promises the mouse that they will marry. Jukka's mouse, of course, turns out to possess a charm and enchantment all her own and, at the wedding feast, it is the older brothers who envy Jukka his clever and beautiful bride.

Anholt, Laurence
Camille and the Sunflowers
Barron's, 1994
Ages 6-10, unpaged
ISBN 0-8120-6409-7

Despite the derision of neighbors, a young French boy named Camille befriends the lonely painter—Vincent Van Gogh—who arrives in his town, and comes to admire his unusual paintings. A charming introduction to Western European artistic traditions, this book is beautifully illustrated by the author's delicate watercolors that evoke Van Gogh's style as well as reproductions of Van Gogh's own paintings of the family in the story—his actual neighbors during his stay in the south of France.

Basile, Giambattista
Petrosinella
Illustrated by Diane Stanley
Frederick Warne, 1981
Ages 4-8, unpaged
ISBN 0-7232-6196-2

In this Neapolitan fairy tale, the object of a young pregnant woman's cravings is the parsley in the neighboring ogress's garden. To satisfy her desire, the young mother-to-be promises to give the witch her unborn child. While the long hair used to gain entry to the tower as well as the handsome prince are reminiscent of *Rapunzel*, in this version, the heroine breaks the magic curse with the aid of three enchanted acorns. To complement the story, Diane Stanley has fashioned a series of lovely wash-and-ink drawings reminiscent of 16th century Italian art. Enzo Gianni's *Little Parsley* (Simon & Schuster, 1991: ISBN 0-671-67197-9) is another retelling of this story.

Bunting, Eve
Clancy's Coat
Illustrated by Lorinda Bryan Cauley
Frederick Warne, 1984
Ages 4-8, unpaged
ISBN 0-7232-6252-7

Clancy and his neighbor, Tippitt the tailor, have been feuding ever since Tippitt's cow, Bridget, ran amok in

Clancy's vegetable garden. But then Clancy comes to Tippitt's door with an old coat that needs turning. What with one thing and another, Tippitt can't seem to get around to working on Clancy's coat, but he is much quicker to allow their bond of friendship to be mended. The lilting Irish dialogue of this heartwarming tale by children's writer Eve Bunting, originally from Ireland, enhances its charm.

Clement, Claude
The Voice of the Wood
Illustrated by Frederic Clement
Dial Books for Young Readers, 1989
Ages 5-10, unpaged
ISBN 0-8037-0635-9

This fantastical tale unfolds in the mist-shrouded canals and courtyards of 18th century Venice, where a musical instrument maker painstakingly crafts a magnificent cello from the wood of a majestic tree. The old artisan finds a famous cellist to do musical justice to his masterpiece but, as it turns out, the instrument has the power to teach the meaning of true humility to even this lofty and renowned musician. The illustrations of Venetian celebrities clustering behind their masks during the Grand Carnival underscore the subtle moral of the story.

Emberley, Michael
Welcome Back, Sun
Little, Brown, 1993
Ages 5-8, unpaged
ISBN 0-316-23647-0

This story takes place during *murketiden*, the long season of darkness that stretches from September to March in mountainous northern Norway. Every year, when the people of the mountain villages feel they cannot bear one more dreary hour of darkness, they re-enact the long trek of a legendary young Norwegian heroine who climbed the area's tallest peak to try to call the sun back to the people. In *Welcome Back, Sun*, we follow the enthusiastic climb of one young girl and her family as they make their annual pilgrimage up Mount Gusta to greet the first rays of the spring sun. The evocative language and illustrations that become lighter and warmer as the cresting of the sun approaches combine to set a fresh and optimistic tone to this Scandinavian story.

MacGill-Callahan, Sheila
The Children of Lir
Illustrated by Gennady Spirin
Dial Books for Young Readers, 1993
Ages 6-10, unpaged
ISBN 0-8037-1121-2

Loosely based on an Irish myth, *The Children of Lir* puts a Gaelic spin on the wicked stepmother stereotype, as the King of Lir's childless second wife is consumed by jealousy over the two sets of twins born to her husband's first queen. She casts a spell over the four youths, transforming them into a quartet of beautiful and mournful-voiced white swans. The queen vows that they will remain in this form until the impossible happens—the two mountain peaks bordering their father's kingdom are joined. The tale of the breaking of the curse by the swans and their friends in the kingdom of nature unfolds against a backdrop of beautifully detailed and magically luminous illustrations by the Russian children's illustrator Gennady Spirin. The book includes a very helpful pronunciation guide to the traditional Irish names.

MacGrory, Yvonne
The Secret of the Ruby Ring
Milkweed Editions, 1994
Ages 9-12, 192 pp.
ISBN 0-915943-92-1

When she makes a wish on a special ring, 11-year-old Lucy McLaughlin is transported from her pampered contemporary life to 1885 Ireland, a turbulent time of land evictions and boycotts. Lucy finds that she is a servant working for a wealthy family. Winner of the 1991 Book of the Year Award from the Irish Children's Book Trust, this exciting story interweaves historical events with a suspenseful plot that will keep readers turning the pages to find out whether Lucy finds her way back through time or remains trapped forever in a bygone era.

Martin, Claire
Boots and the Glass Mountain
Illustrated by Gennady Spirin
Dial Books for Young Readers, 1992
Ages 4-8, unpaged
ISBN 0-8037-1110-7

Based on a Norwegian fairy tale, this story tells how Boots steps in and saves his father's grain fields from the ravages of the trolls' magical wild stallions on Midsummer Night. Then, with the help of the horses, he succeeds in riding up the inaccessible glass mountain and winning the princess's hand in marriage. Lavish illustrations that show curious trolls peeping out from various nooks and crannies complement this classic story.

Nimmo, Jenny
The Starlight Cloak
Illustrated by Justin Todd
Dial Books for Young Readers, 1993
Ages 5-8, unpaged
ISBN 0-8037-1508-0

Another addition to the array of Cinderella stories that exist in various cultures, *The Starlight Cloak* is a traditional Celtic version of this universal tale of the triumph of good over evil. Oona, the young Irish princess, leads a miserable life with her two domineering stepsisters until her foster mother reveals the magical powers hidden in her mysteriously glittering cloak. In this version, Oona and her prince must endure the stepsisters' attempts at revenge before the timeless, happy ending is reached.

Rosen, Billi
Andi's War
Faber & Faber Paperbacks, 1988
Ages 12-16, 136 pp.
ISBN 0-5771-15341-0

Set on an island in the Aegean, *Andi's War* is the story of a young girl's involvement in the civil war between the communist partisans and the monarchists as they fight for control of Greece after World War II. With tensions running high, even the town's children are forced to take sides in the conflict. Antigone (Andi) first finds herself taunted for being a communist by the police chief's son, then watches as childhood mischief and pranks escalate into outright violence. *Andi's War* is a sobering and intensely personal portrayal of the effects of hatred and battle on childhood and family.

The sequel, in which Andi and her father make a new life for themselves in Sweden, is titled *The Other Side of the Mountain* (Faber & Faber Paperbacks, 1990: ISBN 0-571-14190-0).

Schwartz, David M.
Supergrandpa
Illustrated by Bert Dodson
Lothrop, Lee & Shepard, 1991
Ages 4-10, unpaged
ISBN 0-688-09898-3

In 1951, 66-year-old Gustaf Hakansson defied the judges who denied him entrance and rode 1,761 kilometres to the finish line of the Sverige-Loppet, the longest bicycle race in Swedish history. What's more, Hakansson finished first, beating out dozens of younger, more muscular men! *Supergrandpa* is a fictionalized retelling of this story, in which Hakansson's determination and courage helped him beat the odds in a race that nobody believed he had the stamina to finish, let alone win. As a result of his victory, Hakansson became a national hero and legendary figure in Sweden. To this day, Swedish parents encourage their children by saying, "Va' som Stalfarfar"—"Be like Supergrandpa." The pleasant watercolor illustrations capture the timeless look of rural Sweden as the racers streak through thatched villages and along winding country roads.

Strangis, Joel
Grandfather's Rock: An Italian Folktale
Illustrated by Ruth Gamper
Houghton Mifflin, 1993
Ages 4-8, unpaged
ISBN 0-395-65367-3

A poor family in southern Italy brings the children's elderly grandfather to live with them, as he can no longer manage on his own. With winter coming soon, Mother sadly announces that there will not be enough food to feed them all, and it's decided that Grandfather must be sent to live in a home for old people. As the family dejectedly trudges with Grandpa toward the home, Prima, the eldest daughter, realizes that it is up to her to save Grandfather from his dismal fate. This humorous tale of intergenerational family bonding is prettily illustrated with simple watercolor sketches of the Italian countryside.

Indexes

Index—Authors

Afanasyev, Alexander Nikolayevich
  The Fool and the Fish 92

Agard, John
  The Calypso Alphabet 70

Agard, John & Grace Nichols, Eds.
  A Caribbean Dozen: Poems from Caribbean Poets 70

Akio, Terumasa
  Me and Alves: A Japanese Journey 112

Alexander, Lloyd
  The Fortune-Tellers 57
  The Remarkable Journey of Prince Jen 87

Alexander, Sue
  Nadia the Willful 135

Aliki
  The Eggs: A Greek Folktale 169
  Three Gold Pieces 169

Allen, Linda
  The Mouse Bride 169

Ancona, George
  The Piñata Maker/El Piñatero 81

Andrews, Jan
  Very Last First Time 64

Anholt, Laurence
  Camille and the Sunflowers 170

Anno, Mitsumasa
  All in a Day 158

Appiah, Sonia
  Amoko and Efua Bear 57

Ashabranner, Brent
  Gavriel and Jemal: Two Boys of Jerusalem 135

Ashabranner, Brent & Melissa Ashabranner
　Into a Strange Land: Unaccompanied Refugee Youth
　　in America 50

Ashley, Bernard
　Cleversticks 26

Atkin, S. Beth
　Voices from the Fields: Children of Migrant Farmworkers Tell
　　Their Stories 33

Axworthy, Anni
　Anni's India Diary 144

Ayres, Becky Hickox
　Matreshka 92

Bachrach, Susan D.
　Tell Them We Remember: The Story of the Holocaust 121

Bannatyne-Cugnet, Jo & Yvette Moore
　A Prairie Alphabet 64

Barker, Carol
　Ananda in Sri Lanka: A Story of Buddhism 144

Barry, David
　The Rajah's Rice 145

Bartone, Elisa
　Peppe the Lamplighter 30

Basile, Giambattista
　Petrosinella 170

Battle-Lavert, Gwendolyn
　The Barber's Cutting Edge 13

Beatty, Patricia
　Lupita Mañana 33

Bell, William
　Absolutely Invincible 50

Berry, James
　Ajeemah and His Son 71
　The Future-Telling Lady 71

Bial, Raymond
　Amish Home *31*

Bider, Djemma
　A Drop of Honey *136*

Birch, David
　The King's Chessboard *145*

Blanco, Alberta
　Angel's Kite *81*

Boholm-Olsson, Eva
　Tuan *151*

Bond, Ruskin
　Cherry Tree *145*

Bonners, Susan
　The Wooden Doll *30*

Bouchard, David
　If You're Not from the Prairie... *65*

Brett, Jan
　The Mitten *93*

Brown, Tricia
　Chinese New Year *29*

Bruchac, Joseph
　Fox Song *104*

Bryan, Ashley
　The Dancing Granny *72*
　Turtle Knows Your Name *71*

Bunting, Eve
　Clancy's Coat *170*
　Smoky Night *13*

Buss, Fran Leeper
　Journey of the Sparrows *33*

Caduto, Michael J. & Joseph Bruchac
　The Native Stories from Keepers of the Earth *104*

Cameron, Ann
　The Most Beautiful Place in the World *81*

Carlstrom, Nancy White
  Baby-O 72

Carrier, Roch
  The Hockey Sweater 65

Carrison, Muriel Paskin
  Cambodian Folk Stories from the Gatiloke 151

Castañeda, Omar S.
  Abuela's Weave 82
  Among the Volcanoes 83
  Imagining Isabel 83

Choi, Sook Nyul
  Echoes of the White Giraffe 130
  Halmoni and the Picnic 45
  Year of Impossible Goodbyes 130

Cisneros, Sandra
  Hairs—Pelitos 34

Clement, Claude
  The Voice of the Wood 171

Climo, Shirley
  The Korean Cinderella 130

Coerr, Eleanor
  Mieko and the Fifth Treasure 112
  Sadako 113
  Sadako and the Thousand Paper Cranes 113

Cohen, Barbara
  The Carp in the Bathtub 121
  Make a Wish, Molly 122
  Molly's Pilgrim 122
  Yussel's Prayer 122

Crew, Linda
  Children of the River 51

Dawson, Mildred Leinweber
  Over Here It's Different: Carolina's Story 34

De Zutter, Hank
  Who Says a Dog Goes Bow-Wow? 158

Delacre, Lulu
   Arroz con Leche: Popular Songs and Rhymes from Latin America 86

Dolphin, Laurie
   Georgia to Georgia: Making Friends in the U.S.S.R. 93
   Neve Shalom/Wahat al-Salam: Oasis of Peace 136

Dooley, Norah
   Everybody Cooks Rice 159

Dorris, Michael
   Morning Girl 105

Dorros, Arthur
   Abuela 35
   Radio Man: A Story in English and Spanish 35
   This Is My House 159
   Tonight Is Carnaval 83

Doyle, Brian
   Spud Sweetgrass 66

Drucker, Olga Levy
   Kindertransport 123

Edwards, Michelle
   Chicken Man 137

Ehlert, Lois
   Moon Rope: A Peruvian Folktale 84

Emberley, Michael
   Welcome Back, Sun 171

Fairman, Tony
   Bury My Bones but Keep My Words 58

Feelings, Muriel & Tom Feelings
   Jambo Means Hello 61
   Moja Means One 61

Feelings, Tom
   Soul Looks Back in Wonder 14

Filipovic, Zlata
   Zlata's Diary: A Child's Life in Sarajevo 94

Fisher, Leonard Everett
   Alphabet Art: Thirteen ABCs from around the World *160*

Garland, Sherry
   The Lotus Seed *51*
   Song of the Buffalo Boy *152*

Garza, Carmen Lomas
   Family Pictures/Cuadros de Familia *36*

Gavin, Jamila
   The Wheel of Surya *146*

Gershator, Phillis
   The Iroko-Man *58*
   Rata-pata-scata-fata *72*
   Tukama Tootles the Flute: A Tale from the Antilles *72*

Gianni, Enzo
   Little Parsley *170*

Giblin, James Cross
   From Hand to Mouth: Or How We Invented Knives, Forks, Spoons, and Chopsticks and the Table Manners to Go with Them *160*

Gilman, Phoebe
   Something from Nothing *123*

Gilmore, Rachna
   Lights for Gita *48*

Gilson, Jamie
   Hello, My Name Is Scrambled Eggs *51*

Ginsburg, Mirra
   The Chinese Mirror *131*

Girard, Linda Walvoord
   We Adopted You, Benjamin Koo *45*

Goble, Paul
   Love Flute *105*

Godden, Rumer
   Great Grandfather's House *114*

Gogol, Nikolai
   The Nose *94*

Goldfarb, Mace
   Fighters, Refugees, Immigrants: A Story of the Hmong *52*

Gonzalez, Lucia G.
   The Bossy Gallito/El Gallo de Bodas *73*

Gordon, Ginger
   My Two Worlds *36*

Grauer, Rita
   Vasalisa and Her Magic Doll *103*

Greenfeld, Howard
   The Hidden Children *123*

Grifalconi, Ann
   Flyaway Girl *59*
   The Village of Round and Square Houses *59*

Grover, Wayne
   Ali and the Golden Eagle *137*

Gunning, Monica
   Not a Copper Penny in Me House *74*

Hamanaka, Sheila
   All the Colors of the Earth *160*

Hamilton, Virginia
   Drylongso *15*
   Many Thousand Gone *14*
   The People Could Fly *15*

Han, Oki S. & Stephanie Plunkett
   Sir Whong and the Golden Pig *131*

Han, Suzanne Crowder
   Korean Folk and Fairy Tales *132*

Harrison, Ted
   O Canada! *66*

Haskins, Jim
   Count Your Way through Korea *132*

Hausman, Gerald
 Turtle Island ABC: A Gathering of Native American Symbols *106*

Havill, Juanita
 Treasure Nap *37*

Heide, Florence Parry & Judith Heide Gilliland
 Sami and the Time of the Troubles *138*
 The Day of Ahmed's Secret *138*

Hesse, Karen
 Letters from Rivka *125*

Hicyilmaz, Gaye
 Against the Storm *139*
 The Frozen Waterfall *139*

Higa, Tomiko
 The Girl with the White Flag *114*

Hill, Lawrence
 Trials and Triumphs: The Story of African-Canadians *15*

Hirsh, Marilyn
 Joseph Who Loved the Sabbath *125*

Ho, Minfong
 The Clay Marble *152*
 Rice without Rain *153*

Hobbs, Will
 Bearstone *106*

Hoberman, Mary Ann, Ed.
 My Song Is Beautiful: Poems and Pictures in Many Voices *161*

Hodge, Merle
 For the Life of Laetitia *74*

Hodges, Margaret
 The Golden Deer *146*

Hoffman, Mary
 Amazing Grace *16*

Hong, Lily Toy
   How the Ox Star Fell from Heaven *88*
   Two of Everything *87*

Hopkinson, Deborah
   Sweet Clara and the Freedom Quilt *16*

Howlett, Bud
   I'm New Here *37*

Hoyt-Goldsmith, Diane
   Pueblo Storyteller *107*

Hudson, Wade, Ed.
   Pass It On: African-American Poetry for Children *17*

Huynh, Quang Nhuong
   The Land I Lost: Adventures of a Boy in Vietnam *153*

Irwin, Hadley
   Kim/Kimi *41*

Isadora, Rachel
   At the Crossroads *59*

Ishii, Momoko
   The Tongue-Cut Sparrow *115*

Jaffe, Nina
   Patakin: World Tales of Drums and Drummers *161*

Jaffrey, Madhur
   Seasons of Splendour: Tales, Myths and Legends of India *146*

Jennss, Aylette
   Come Home with Me: A Multicultural Treasure Hunt *162*

Johnson, Angela
   The Leaving Morning *18*
   Toning the Sweep *17*

Johnston, Tony
   The Old Lady and the Birds *84*

Joseph, Lynn
   Coconut Kind of Day: Island Poems *75*
   A Wave in Her Pocket: Stories from Trinidad *75*

Keegan, Marcia
   Pueblo Boy: Growing Up in Two Worlds *107*

Keens-Douglas, Richardo
   La Diablesse and the Baby *75*
   The Nutmeg Princess *76*

Keller, Holly
   Island Baby *76*
   Grandfather's Dream *153*

Kendall, Russ
   Russian Girl: Life in an Old Russian Town *95*

Kherdian, David
   Feathers and Tails: Animal Fables from around the World *162*

Kimmel, Eric
   The Three Princes: A Tale from the Middle East *140*

Kismaric, Carole
   The Rumor of Pavel and Paali *95*

Kline, Suzy
   Song Lee in Room 2B *46*

Knight, Margy Burns
   Talking Walls *162*
   Welcoming Babies *163*

Kogawa, Joy
   Naomi's Road *41*

Kurtz, Jane
   Fire on the Mountain *60*

Laird, Elizabeth
   Kiss the Dust *140*

Langton, Jane
   Salt: A Russian Folktale *96*

Lankford, Mary D.
   Hopscotch around the World *163*

Lauture, Denize
   Father and Son *18*

Lawrence, Jacob
   The Great Migration: An American Story *18*

Lee, Huy Voun
   At the Beach *88*

Lee, Jeanne M.
   Ba-Nam *154*
   Legend of the Milky Way *98*

Lee, Marie G.
   Finding My Voice *46*
   If It Hadn't been for Yoon Jun *46*
   Saying Goodbye *47*

Leigh, Nila K.
   Learning to Swim in Swaziland: A Child's-Eye View of a Southern African Country *60*

Leitner, Isabella
   The Big Lie *126*

Lerner Publications Staff
   Ukraine Then and Now *96*

Lessac, Frané
   The Little Island *77*

Lessac, Frané, Ed.
   Caribbean Canvas *76*

Levine, Arthur A.
   The Boy Who Drew Cats: A Japanese Folktale *115*

Levine, Ellen
   I Hate English! *26*

Lim, Sing
   West Coast Chinese Boy *27*

Linden, Ann Marie
   One Smiling Grandma: A Caribbean Counting Book *77*

Littlechild, George
   This Land Is My Land *108*

London, Jonathan
   Fire Race: A Karuk Coyote Tale *108*

Lord, Bette Bao
   In the Year of the Boar and Jackie Robinson 27
Louie, Ai-Ling
   Yeh-Shen 89
Lowry, Lois
   Number the Stars 126
MacGill-Callahan, Sheila
   The Children of Lir 172
MacGrory, Yvonne
   The Secret of the Ruby Ring 172
Manson, Christopher
   A Gift for the King: A Persian Tale 140
Margolies, Barbara A.
   Rehema's Journey: A Visit in Tanzania 61
Markun, Patricia Maloney
   The Little Painter of Sabana Grande 84
Martin, Claire
   Boots and the Glass Mountain 173
Martin, Rafe
   The Rough-Face Girl 109
Marton, Jirina
   You Can Go Home Again 97
Matas, Carol
   Sworn Enemies 127
Mathieson, Feroza
   The Very Special Sari 147
McFarlane, Sheryl
   Waiting for the Whales 66
McGugan, Jim
   Josepha: A Prairie Boy's Story 67
McKissack, Patricia C.
   The Dark Thirty: Southern Tales of the Supernatural 19
   Mirandy and Brother Wind 19

McMahon, Patricia
   Chi-Hoon: A Korean Girl *133*

Means, Florence Crannell
   The Moved-Outers *42*

Meeker, Clare Hodgson
   A Tale of Two Rice Birds *154*

Meyer, Carolyn
   Rio Grande Stories *164*

Mikaelson, Ben
   Sparrow Hawk Red *38*

Mitchell, Margaree King
   Uncle Jed's Barbershop *20*

Mitchell, Rita Phillips
   Hue Boy *77*

Mochizuki, Ken
   Baseball Saved Us *42*

Mollel, Tololwa M.
   The Orphan Boy *61*

Momiji Health Care Society
   Baachan! Geechan! Arigato *42*

Mora, Pat
   Listen to the Desert/Oye al Desierto *38*

Morgan, Allen
   The Magic Hockey Skates *67*

Mori, Kyoko
   Shizuko's Daughter *117*

Moroney, Lynn
   Elinda Who Danced in the Sky: An Estonian
     Folktale *97*

Morris, Ann
   Houses and Homes *164*

Myers, Walter Dean
   Brown Angels *20*

Naidoo, Beverley
  Chain of Fire *62*
  Journey to Jo'burg: A South African Story *62*

Namioka, Lensey
  Yang the Youngest and His Terrible Ear *28*
  Yang the Third and Her Impossible Family *28*

Newton, Pam
  The Stonecutter *147*

Nikola-Lisa, W.
  Bein' with You This Way *165*

Nimmo, Jenny
  The Starlight Cloak *173*

Nomura, Takaaki
  Grandpa's Town *116*

Nye, Naomi Shihab
  The Same Sky: A Collection of Poems from around the World *165*
  Sitti's Secrets *141*

O'Brien, Anne Sibley
  The Princess and the Beggar: A Korean Folktale *133*

Oberman, Sheldon
  The Always Prayer Shawl *127*

Orozco, José-Luis
  De Colores and Other Latin-American Folk Songs for Children *85*

Orr, Katherine
  My Grandpa and the Sea *78*

Osborne, Mary Pope
  Mermaid Tales from around the World *166*

Paek, Min
  Aekyung's Dream *47*

Palacek, Libuse & Josef
  The Magic Grove *142*

Parry, Caroline
  Let's Celebrate! Canada's Special Days *166*

Paulsen, Gary
　Nightjohn 21

Perkins, Mitali
　The Sunita Experiment 48

Pevear, Richard
　Our King Has Horns! 98

Philip, Marlene Nourbese
　Harriet's Daughter 78

Polacco, Patricia
　Just Plain Fancy 31
　Mrs. Katz and Tush 21
　Rechenka's Eggs 98
　Tikvah Means Hope 128

Pomerantz, Charlotte
　The Tamarindo Puppy and Other Poems 85

Poulin, Stéphane
　Ah! Belle cité! A Beautiful City 68

Prochazkova, Iva
　The Season of Secret Wishes 99

Rattigan, Jama Kim
　Dumpling Soup 166

Reddix, Valerie
　Dragon Kite of the Autumn Moon 89

Rhee, Nami
　Magic Spring: A Korean Folktale 134

Rhoads, Dorothy
　The Corn Grows Ripe 109

Ringgold, Faith
　Aunt Harriet's Underground Railroad in the Sky 23
　Dinner at Aunt Connie's House 22
　Tar Beach 22

Robinson, Marc & Steve Jenkins
　Cock-A-Doodle-Doo! What Does It Sound Like to You? 158

Rodanas, Kristina
　The Story of Wali Dad　*148*

Roop, Peter & Connie Roop
　Ahyoka and the Talking Leaves　*110*

Rose, Deborah Lee
　The People Who Hugged the Trees　*148*

Rosen, Billi
　Andi's War　*173*
　The Other Side of the Mountain　*174*

Rosen, Michael J.
　Elijah's Angel　*128*

Rosen, Michael, Ed.
　South and North, East and West: The Oxfam Book
　　of Children's Stories　*167*

Roth, Susan L.
　Buddha　*148*

Sadlier, Rosemary
　Leading the Way: Black Women in Canada　*23*

San Souci, Robert D.
　The Samurai's Daughter　*117*
　Sukey and the Mermaid　*23*

Say, Allen
　Grandfather's Journey　*43*
　Tree of Cranes　*117*

Schami, Rafik
　A Hand Full of Stars　*142*

Schlein, Miriam
　The Year of the Panda　*90*

Schwartz, David M.
　Supergrandpa　*174*

Service, Robert W.
　The Cremation of Sam McGee　*68*
　The Shooting of Dan McGrew　*69*

Seymour, Tryntje Van Ness
　The Gift of Changing Woman　*110*

Shalant, Phyllis
　Look What We've Brought You from Vietnam *155*

Shepard, Aaron
　Savriti: A Tale of Ancient India *149*

Shute, Linda
　Momotaro the Peach Boy *117*

Singer, Marilyn
　Nine O'Clock Lullaby *167*

Sis, Peter
　A Small Tall Tale from the Far Far North *99*
　The Three Golden Keys *100*

Snyder, Dianne
　The Boy of the Three-Year Nap *118*

Soto, Gary
　Baseball in April and Other Stories *39*
　Too Many Tamales *39*

Stanley, Diane
　Fortune *143*

Staples, Suzanne Fisher
　Haveli *150*
　Shabanu: Daughter of the Wind *149*

Stock, Catherine
　Where Are You Going, Manyoni? *63*

Stone, Susheila
　Nadeem Makes Samosas *49*

Strangis, Joel
　Grandfather's Rock: An Italian Folktale *174*

Surat, Michele Maria
　Angel Child, Dragon Child *53*

Tagore, Rabindrath
　Paper Boats *150*

Taylor, Allegra
　A Kibbutz in Israel *143*

Taylor, C.J.
  How Two-Feather Was Saved from Loneliness: An Abenaki Legend *111*

Temple, Frances
  Taste of Salt *79*

Terzian, Alexandra M.
  The Kids' Multicultural Art Book: Art and Craft Experiences from around the World *168*

Thomas, Jane Resh
  Lights on the River *40*

Thomas, Joyce Carol
  Brown Honey in Broomwheat Tea *14*

Tompert, Ann
  Bamboo Hats and a Rice Cake *118*

Torres, Leyla
  Subway Sparrow *168*

Tran, Khanh-Tuyet
  The Little Weaver of Thai-Yen Village *53*

Trivas, Irene
  Annie...Anya *100*

Tundra Books
  Canadian Childhoods *69*

Uchida, Yoshiko
  The Best Bad Thing *44*
  The Bracelet *43*
  The Happiest Ending *44*
  A Jar of Dreams *44*
  Journey to Topaz *41*

UNICEF
  I Dream of Peace *101*

Ushinsky, Constantin
  How a Shirt Grew in the Field *101*

Vagin, Vladimir & Franck Asch
  Here Comes the Cat! *102*

van der Rol, Ruud & Rian Verhoeven
    Anne Frank—Beyond the Diary: A Photographic
        Remembrance *129*

Vuong, Lynette Dyer
    The Brocaded Slipper and Other Vietnamese Tales *156*
    The Golden Carp and Other Tales from Vietnam *155*
    Sky Legends of Vietnam *155*

Wall, Lina Mao & Cathy Spagnoli
    Judge Rabbit and the Tree Spirit: A Folktale
        from Cambodia *156*

Wallace, Ian
    Chin Chiang and the Dragon's Dance *28*

Wallace, Ian & Angela Wood
    The Sandwich *31*

Wartski, Maureen Crane
    A Boat to Nowhere *54*
    A Long Way from Home *54*

Waters, Kate & Madeline Slovenz Low
    Lion Dancer: Ernie Wan's Chinese New Year *28*

Watkins, Yoko Kawashima
    My Brother, My Sister and I *119*
    So Far from the Bamboo Grove *119*
    Tales from the Bamboo Grove *119*

Wells, Ruth
    A to Zen: A Book of Japanese Culture *120*

Whelan, Gloria
    Goodbye Vietnam *54*

Wild, Margaret
    A Time for Toys *129*

Williams, Karen Lynn
    Galimoto *62*
    Tap-Tap *79*

Winter, Jeanette
    Diego *86*
    Follow the Drinking Gourd *24*
    Klara's New World *32*

Winthrop, Elizabeth
  Vasilissa the Beautiful *102*

Wisniewski, David
  Sundiata, Lion King of Mali *63*

Wolkstein, Diane
  The Magic Orange Tree and Other Haitian Folktales *80*
  Oom Razoom or Go I Know Not Where, Bring Back
    I Know Not What *103*

Woodson, Jacqueline
  Last Summer with Maizon *24*
  Maizon at Blue Hill *25*

Xiong, Blia
  Nine-in-One, Grr! Grr! *156*

Yagawa, Sumiko
  The Crane Wife *119*

Yarbrough, Camille
  Cornrows *25*

Yee, Paul
  Roses Sing on New Snow *29*

Yep, Laurence
  The Rainbow People *90*
  The Star Fisher *29*

Young, Ed
  Lon Po Po *90*

Zhensun, Zheng & Alice Low
  A Young Painter: The Life and Paintings of Wang Yani *91*

Zucker, David
  Uncle Carmello *32*

Index—Titles

A to Zen: A Book of Japanese Culture *120*
Absolutely Invincible *50*
Abuela *35*
Abuela's Weave *82*
Aekyung's Dream *47*
Against the Storm *139*
Ah! Belle cité! A Beautiful City *68*
Ahyoka and the Talking Leaves *110*
Ajeemah and His Son *71*
Ali and the Golden Eagle *137*
All in a Day *158*
All the Colors of the Earth *160*
Alphabet Art: Thirteen ABCs from around the World *160*
The Always Prayer Shawl *127*
Amazing Grace *16*
Amish Home *31*
Amoko and Efua Bear *57*
Among the Volcanoes *83*
Ananda in Sri Lanka: A Story of Buddhism *144*
Andi's War *173*
Angel Child, Dragon Child *53*
Angel's Kite *81*
Anne Frank—Beyond the Diary: A Photographic Remembrance *129*
Anni's India Diary *144*
Annie...Anya *100*
Arroz con Leche: Popular Songs and Rhymes from Latin America *86*
At the Beach *88*
At the Crossroads *59*
Aunt Harriet's Underground Railroad in the Sky *23*
Ba-Nam *154*
Baachan! Geechan! Arigato *42*
Baby-O *72*
Bamboo Hats and a Rice Cake *118*
The Barber's Cutting Edge *13*
Baseball in April and Other Stories *39*
Baseball Saved Us *42*

199

Bearstone *106*
Bein' with You This Way *165*
The Best Bad Thing *44*
The Big Lie *126*
A Boat to Nowhere *54*
Boots and the Glass Mountain *173*
The Bossy Gallito/El Gallo de Bodas *73*
The Boy of the Three-Year Nap *118*
The Boy Who Drew Cats: A Japanese Folktale *115*
The Bracelet *43*
Bread, Bread, Bread *165*
The Brocaded Slipper and Other Vietnamese Tales *156*
Brown Angels *20*
Brown Honey in Broomwheat Tea *14*
Buddha *148*
Bury My Bones but Keep My Words *58*
The Calypso Alphabet *70*
Cambodian Folk Stories from the Gatiloke *151*
Camille and the Sunflowers *170*
Canadian Childhoods *69*
Caribbean Canvas *76*
A Caribbean Dozen: Poems from Caribbean Poets *70*
The Carp in the Bathtub *121*
Chain of Fire *62*
Cherry Tree *145*
Chi-Hoon: A Korean Girl *133*
Chicken Man *137*
The Children of Lir *172*
Children of the River *51*
Chin Chiang and the Dragon's Dance *28*
The Chinese Mirror *131*
Chinese New Year *29*
Clancy's Coat *170*
The Clay Marble *152*
Cleversticks *26*
Cock-A-Doodle-Doo! What Does It Sound Like to You? *158*
Coconut Kind of Day: Island Poems *75*
Come Home with Me: A Multicultural Treasure Hunt *162*
The Corn Grows Ripe *109*
Cornrows *25*
Count Your Way through Korea *132*
The Crane Wife *120*

The Cremation of Sam McGee *68*
The Dancing Granny *72*
The Dark Thirty: Southern Tales of the Supernatural *19*
The Day of Ahmed's Secret *138*
De Colores and Other Latin-American Folk Songs
   for Children *85*
Diego *86*
Dinner at Aunt Connie's House *22*
Dragon Kite of the Autumn Moon *89*
A Drop of Honey *136*
Drylongso *15*
Dumpling Soup *166*
Echoes of the White Giraffe *130*
The Eggs: A Greek Folktale *169*
Elijah's Angel *128*
Elinda Who Danced in the Sky: An Estonian Folktale *97*
Everybody Cooks Rice *159*
Family Pictures/Cuadros de Familia *36*
Father and Son *18*
Feathers and Tails: Animal Fables from around the World *162*
Fighters, Refugees, Immigrants: A Story of the Hmong *52*
Finding My Voice *46*
Fire on the Mountain *60*
Fire Race: A Karuk Coyote Tale *108*
Flyaway Girl *59*
Follow the Drinking Gourd *24*
The Fool and the Fish *92*
For the Life of Laetitia *74*
Fortune *143*
The Fortune-Tellers *57*
Fox Song *104*
From Hand to Mouth: Or How We Invented Knives, Forks,
   Spoons and Chopsticks and the Table Manners to Go
   with Them *160*
The Frozen Waterfall *139*
The Future-Telling Lady *71*
Galimoto *62*
Gavriel and Jemal: Two Boys of Jerusalem *135*
Georgia to Georgia: Making Friends in the U.S.S.R. *93*
A Gift for the King: A Persian Tale *141*
The Gift of Changing Woman *110*
The Girl with the White Flag *114*

The Golden Carp and Other Tales from Vietnam *155*
The Golden Deer *146*
Goodbye Vietnam *54*
Grandfather's Dream *153*
Grandfather's Journey *43*
Grandfather's Rock: An Italian Folktale *174*
Grandpa's Town *116*
Great Grandfather's House *114*
The Great Migration: An American Story *18*
Hairs—Pelitos *34*
Halmoni and the Picnic *45*
A Hand Full of Stars *142*
The Happiest Ending *44*
Harriet's Daughter *78*
Hats, Hats, Hats *165*
Haveli *150*
Hello, My Name Is Scrambled Eggs *52*
Here Comes the Cat! *102*
The Hidden Children *124*
The Hockey Sweater *65*
Hopscotch around the World *163*
The House on Mango Street *34*
Houses and Homes *164*
How a Shirt Grew in the Field *101*
How the Ox Star Fell from Heaven *88*
How Two-Feather Was Saved from Loneliness: An Abenaki Legend *111*
How We Saw the World: Nine Native Stories of of the Way Things Began *111*
Hue Boy *77*
I Dream of Peace *101*
I Hate English! *26*
I'm New Here *37*
If It Hadn't Been for Yoon Jun *46*
If You're Not from the Prairie... *65*
Imagining Isabel *83*
In the Year of the Boar and Jackie Robinson *27*
Into a Strange Land: Unaccompanied Refugee Youth in America *50*
The Iroko-Man: A Yoruba Folktale *58*
Island Baby *76*
Jambo Means Hello *61*

A Jar of Dreams *44*
Joseph Who Loved the Sabbath *125*
Josepha: A Prairie Boy's Story *67*
Journey of the Sparrows *33*
Journey to Jo'burg: A South African Story *62*
Journey to Topaz *41*
Judge Rabbit and the Tree Spirit: A Folktale from Cambodia *156*
Just Plain Fancy *31*
A Kibbutz in Israel *143*
The Kids' Multicultural Art Book: Art and Craft Experiences from around the World *168*
Kim/Kimi *41*
Kindertransport *123*
The King's Chessboard *145*
Kiss the Dust *140*
Klara's New World *32*
The Korean Cinderella *130*
Korean Folk and Fairy Tales *132*
La Diablesse and the Baby *75*
The Land I Lost: Adventures of a Boy in Vietnam *153*
Last Summer with Maizon *24*
Leading the Way: Black Women in Canada *23*
Learning to Swim in Swaziland: A Child's-Eye View of a Southern African Country *60*
The Leaving Morning *18*
Legend of the Milky Way *98*
Let's Celebrate! Canada's Special Days *166*
Letters from Rivka *125*
Lights for Gita *48*
Lights on the River *40*
Lion Dancer: Ernie Wan's Chinese New Year *28*
Listen to the Desert/Oye al Desierto *38*
The Little Island *77*
The Little Painter of Sabana Grande *84*
Little Parsley *170*
The Little Weaver of Thai-Yen Village *53*
Lon Po Po *90*
A Long Way from Home *54*
Look What We've Brought You from Vietnam *155*
The Lotus Seed *51*
Love Flute *105*
Loving *165*

Lupita Mañana 33
The Magic Grove 142
The Magic Hockey Skates 67
The Magic Orange Tree and Other Haitian Folktales 80
Magic Spring: A Korean Folktale 134
Maizon at Blue Hill 25
Make a Wish, Molly 122
Many Thousand Gone 14
Manzur Goes to the Airport 49
Matreshka 92
Me and Alves: A Japanese Journey 112
Mermaid Tales from around the World 166
Mieko and the Fifth Treasure 112
Mirandy and Brother Wind 19
The Mitten 93
Moja Means One 61
Molly's Pilgrim 122
Momotaro the Peach Boy 117
Moon Rope: A Peruvian Folktale 84
Morning Girl 105
The Most Beautiful Place in the World 81
The Mouse Bride 169
The Moved-Outers 42
Mrs. Katz and Tush 21
My Brother, My Sister and I 119
My Grandpa and the Sea 78
My Song Is Beautiful: Poems and Pictures in Many Voices 161
My Two Worlds 36
Nadeem Makes Samosas 49
Nadia the Willful 135
Naomi's Road 41
The Native Stories from Keepers of the Earth 104
Neve Shalom/Wahat al-Salam: Oasis of Peace 136
Nightjohn 21
Nine O'Clock Lullaby 167
Nine-in-One, Grr! Grr! 156
The Nose 94
Not a Copper Penny in Me House 74
Number the Stars 126
The Nutmeg Princess 76
O Canada! 66
The Old Lady and the Birds 84

On the Go *165*
One Smiling Grandma: A Caribbean Counting Book *77*
Oom Razoom or Go I Know Not Where, Bring Back I Know Not What *103*
The Orphan Boy *61*
The Other Side of the Mountain *174*
Our King Has Horns! *98*
Over Here It's Different: Carolina's Story *34*
Paper Boats *150*
Pass It On: African-American Poetry for Children *17*
Patakin: World Tales of Drums and Drummers *161*
The People Could Fly *15*
The People Who Hugged the Trees *148*
Peppe the Lamplighter *30*
The Perfect Present *147*
Petrosinella *170*
The Piñata Maker/El Piñatero *81*
A Prairie Alphabet *64*
The Princess and the Beggar: A Korean Folktale *133*
Pueblo Boy: Growing Up in Two Worlds *107*
Pueblo Storyteller *107*
Radio Man: A Story in English and Spanish *35*
The Rainbow People *90*
The Rajah's Rice *145*
Ranjit and the Fire Engines *49*
Rata-pata-scata-fata *72*
Rechenka's Eggs *98*
Rehema's Journey: A Visit in Tanzania *61*
The Remarkable Journey of Prince Jen *87*
Rice without Rain *153*
Rio Grande Stories *164*
The Roller Birds of Rampur *49*
Roses Sing on New Snow *29*
The Rough-Face Girl *109*
The Rumor of Pavel and Paali *95*
Russian Girl: Life in an Old Russian Town *95*
Sadako *113*
Sadako and the Thousand Paper Cranes *113*
Salt: A Russian Folktale *96*
Sami and the Time of the Troubles *138*
The Samurai's Daughter *117*
The Sandwich *31*

Savitri: A Tale of Ancient India *149*
Saying Goodbye *47*
The Season of Secret Wishes *99*
Seasons of Splendour: Tales, Myths and Legends of India *146*
The Secret of the Ruby Ring *172*
Shabanu: Daughter of the Wind *149*
Shizuko's Daughter *116*
The Shooting of Dan McGrew *69*
Sir Whong and the Golden Pig *131*
Sitti's Secrets *141*
Sky Legends of Vietnam *155*
A Small Tall Tale from the Far Far North *99*
Smoky Night *13*
So Far from the Bamboo Grove *119*
Something from Nothing *123*
Song Lee in Room 2B *46*
Song of the Buffalo Boy *152*
Soul Looks Back in Wonder *14*
South and North, East and West: The Oxfam Book of Children's Stories *167*
Sparrow Hawk Red *38*
Spud Sweetgrass *66*
The Star Fisher *29*
The Starlight Cloak *173*
The Stonecutter *147*
The Story of Wali Dad *148*
Subway Sparrow *168*
Sukey and the Mermaid *23*
Sundiata, Lion King of Mali *63*
The Sunita Experiment *48*
Supergrandpa *174*
Sweet Clara and the Freedom Quilt *16*
Sworn Enemies *127*
A Tale of Two Rice Birds *154*
Tales from the Bamboo Grove *119*
Talking Walls *162*
The Tamarindo Puppy and Other Poems *85*
Tap-Tap *79*
Tar Beach *22*
Taste of Salt *79*
Tell Them We Remember: The Story of the Holocaust *121*
This Is My House *159*

This Land Is My Land 108
This Same Sky: A Collection of Poems from around
  the World 165
Three Gold Pieces 169
The Three Golden Keys 100
The Three Princes: A Tale from the Middle East 140
Tikvah Means Hope 128
A Time for Toys 129
The Tongue-Cut Sparrow 115
Tonight Is Carnaval 83
Toning the Sweep 17
Too Many Tamales 39
Treasure Nap 37
Tree of Cranes 117
Trials and Triumphs: The Story of African-Canadians 15
Tuan 151
Tukama Tootles the Flute: A Tale from the Antilles 73
Turtle Island ABC: A Gathering of Native American Symbols 106
Turtle Knows Your Name 71
Two of Everything 87
Ukraine Then and Now 96
Uncle Carmello 32
Uncle Jed's Barbershop 20
Vasalisa and Her Magic Doll 103
Vasilissa the Beautiful 102
The Very Hot Samosas 147
Very Last First Time 64
The Very Special Sari 147
The Village of Round and Square Houses 59
The Voice of the Wood 171
Voices from the Fields: Children of Migrant Farmworkers Tell
  Their Stories 33
Waiting for the Whales 66
A Wave in Her Pocket: Stories from Trinidad 75
We Adopted You, Benjamin Koo 45
Welcome Back, Sun 171
Welcoming Babies 162
West Coast Chinese Boy 27
Whatever Next? 147
The Wheel of Surya 146
Where Are You Going, Manyoni? 63
Who Says a Dog Goes Bow-Wow? 158

The Wooden Doll 30
Yang the Youngest and His Terrible Ear 28
Yang the Third and Her Impossible Family 28
Year of Impossible Goodbyes 130
The Year of the Panda 90
Yeh-Shen 89
You Can Go Home Again 97
A Young Painter: The Life and Paintings of Wang Yani 91
Yussel's Prayer 122
Zlata's Diary: A Child's Life in Sarajevo 94

Index—Themes

Across the Generations
  Abuela *35*
  Abuela's Weave *82*
  The Always Prayer Shawl *127*
  Ba-Nam *154*
  Bearstone *106*
  Cherry Tree *145*
  Chin Chiang and the Dragon's Dance *28*
  Dragon Kite of the Autumn Moon *89*
  Elijah's Angel *128*
  Fox Song *104*
  Grandfather's Dream *153*
  Grandfather's Journey *43*
  Grandfather's Rock: An Italian Folktale *174*
  Grandpa's Town *116*
  Great Grandfather's House *114*
  Halmoni and the Picnic *45*
  The Lotus Seed *51*
  Mrs. Katz and Tush *21*
  My Grandpa and the Sea *78*
  One Smiling Grandma: A Caribbean Counting Book *77*
  Pueblo Storyteller *107*
  Sitti's Secrets *141*
  Something from Nothing *123*
  Supergrandpa *174*
  Tikvah Means Hope *128*
  Toning the Sweep *17*
  Uncle Carmello *32*
  Uncle Jed's Barbershop *20*
  Waiting for the Whales *66*
  The Wooden Doll *30*

Alphabet and Counting Books
  A to Zen: A Book of Japanese Culture *120*
  Ah! Belle cité! A Beautiful City *68*
  Alphabet Art: Thirteen ABCs from around the World *159*
  The Calypso Alphabet *70*
  Count your Way through Korea *132*
  Jambo Means Hello *61*

Moja Means One *61*
One Smiling Grandma: A Caribbean Counting Book *77*
A Prairie Alphabet *64*
Turtle Island ABC: A Gathering of Native American Symbols *106*

Animals
Ali and the Golden Eagle *137*
The Bossy Gallito/El Gallo de Bodas *73*
Chicken Man *137*
Feathers and Tails: Animal Fables from around the World *162*
Fire Race: A Karuk Coyote Tale *108*
The Golden Deer *146*
Here Comes the Cat! *102*
Island Baby *76*
Just Plain Fancy *31*
The Land I Lost: Adventures of a Boy in Vietnam *153*
Listen to the Desert/Oye al Desierto *38*
The Magic Grove *142*
The Mitten *93*
The Mouse Bride *169*
Mrs. Katz and Tush *21*
Nine-in-One, Grr! Grr! *156*
The Old Lady and the Birds *84*
Rehema's Journey: A Visit in Tanzania *61*
Tikvah Means Hope *128*
Turtle Knows Your Name *71*
Who Says a Dog Goes Bow-Wow? *158*
The Year of the Panda *90*

The Arts
Alphabet Art: Thirteen ABCs from around the World *159*
At the Beach *88*
The Boy Who Drew Cats: A Japanese Folktale *115*
Camille and the Sunflowers *170*
Canadian Childhoods *69*
Caribbean Canvas *76*
De Colores and Other Latin-American Folk Songs for Children *85*
Diego *86*
Dinner at Aunt Connie's House *22*
The Great Migration: An American Story *18*

I Dream of Peace *101*
The Kids' Multicultural Art Book: Art and Craft Experiences from around the World *168*
The Little Painter of Sabana Grande *84*
Look What We've Brought You from Vietnam *155*
Mieko and the Fifth Treasure *112*
The Old Lady and the Birds *84*
Patakin: World Tales of Drums and Drummers *161*
The Piñata Maker/El Piñatero *81*
Pueblo Storyteller *107*
Rechenka's Eggs *98*
Tar Beach *22*
This Land Is My Land *108*
The Voice of the Wood *171*
West Coast Chinese Boy *27*
Yang the Youngest and His Terrible Ear *28*
A Young Painter: The Life and Paintings of Wang Yani *91*

The Environment
Grandfather's Dream *153*
Island Baby *76*
The Native Stories from Keepers of the Earth *104*
The People Who Hugged the Trees *148*
Turtle Island ABC: A Gathering of Native American Symbols *106*
Welcome Back, Sun *171*
The Year of the Panda *90*

Fairy Tales across Cultures
Boots and the Glass Mountain *173*
The Brocaded Slipper and Other Vietnamese Tales *156*
The Boy Who Drew Cats: A Japanese Folktale *115*
The Children of Lir *172*
The Crane Wife *120*
Elinda Who Danced in the Sky: An Estonian Folktale *97*
Fortune *143*
The Korean Cinderella *130*
Korean Folk and Fairy Tales *132*
La Diablesse and the Baby *75*
Lon Po Po *90*
Mermaid Tales from around the World *166*
The Mouse Bride *169*
Momotaro the Peach Boy *117*

Oom Razoom or Go I Know What Where, Bring Back
   I Know Not What *103*
Petrosinella *170*
The Rough-Face Girl *109*
South and North, East and West: The Oxfam Book
   of Children's Stories *167*
The Starlight Cloak *173*
The Stonecutter *147*
Sukey and the Mermaid *23*
The Three Princes: A Tale from the Middle East *140*
Vasilissa the Beautiful *102*
Yeh-Shen *89*

Family Relationships
Ahyoka and the Talking Leaves *110*
Andi's War *173*
At the Crossroads *59*
Cornrows *25*
Dumpling Soup *167*
Family Pictures/Cuadros de Familia *36*
Father and Son *18*
Finding My Voice *46*
Hairs—Pelitos *34*
Hue Boy *77*
Journey to Jo'burg: A South African Story *62*
Morning Girl *105*
Nadia the Willful *135*
Peppe the Lamplighter *30*
Sami and the Time of the Troubles *138*
The Season of Secret Wishes *99*
Shizuko's Daughter *116*
The Star Fisher *29*
Treasure Nap *37*
Tree of Cranes *117*
Uncle Carmello *32*
We Adopted You, Benjamin Koo *45*
Yang the Youngest and His Terrible Ear *28*
You Can Go Home Again *97*

Food and Nutrition
Bread, Bread, Bread *165*
The Carp in the Bathtub *121*
Cherry Tree *145*

Cleversticks *26*
The Dancing Granny *72*
A Drop of Honey *136*
Dumpling Soup *166*
The Eggs: A Greek Folktale *169*
Everybody Cooks Rice *159*
From Hand to Mouth: Or How We Invented Knives, Forks, Spoons, and Chopsticks and the Table Manners to Go with Them *160*
How the Ox Star Fell from Heaven *88*
Nadeem Makes Samosas *49*
Roses Sing on New Snow *29*
The Sandwich *31*
Too Many Tamales *39*
The Very Hot Samosas *147*
Very Last First Time *64*

Friendship
Absolutely Invincible *50*
Angel Child, Dragon Child *53*
Annie...Anya *100*
The Bracelet *43*
Clancy's Coat *170*
Georgia to Georgia: Making Friends in the U.S.S.R. *93*
A Hand Full of Stars *142*
Here Comes the Cat! *102*
If It Hadn't Been for Yoon Jun *46*
Josepha: A Prairie Boy's Story *67*
Last Summer with Maizon *24*
Lights for Gita *48*
Mirandy and Brother Wind *19*
Mrs. Katz and Tush *21*
The Little Island *77*
Naomi's Road *41*
Number the Stars *126*
Spud Sweetgrass *66*
Tikvah Means Hope *128*
Yang the Youngest and His Terrible Ear *28*

Holidays and Celebrations
Bamboo Hats and a Rice Cake *118*
The Carp in the Bathtub *121*
Chinese New Year *29*

Chin Chiang and the Dragon's Dance 28
De Colores and Other Latin-American Folk Songs
   for Children 85
Dumpling Soup 167
Elijah's Angel 128
Joseph Who Loved the Sabbath 125
Let's Celebrate! Canada's Special Days 166
Lights for Gita 48
Lights on the River 40
Lion Dancer! Ernie Wan's Chinese New Year 28
Make a Wish, Molly 122
Seasons of Splendour: Tales, Myths and Legends
   of India 146
Tonight Is Carnaval 83
Too Many Tamales 39
Tree of Cranes 117
The Very Special Sari 147
Welcoming Babies 162
Yussel's Prayer 122

Immigration and Adjustment
Aekyung's Dream 147
Angel Child, Dragon Child 53
The Frozen Waterfall 139
Halmoni and the Picnic 45
Harriet's Daughter 78
I Hate English! 26
I'm New Here 37
In the Year of the Boar and Jackie Robinson 27
Klara's New World 32
Letters from Rivka 125
Lights for Gita 48
The Lotus Seed 51
Molly's Pilgrim 122
My Two Worlds 36
Over Here It's Different: Carolina's Story 34
The Star Fisher 29
West Coast Chinese Boy 27
Yang the Youngest and His Terrible Ear 28

Poetry
Arroz con Leche: Popular Songs and Rhymes from Latin
   America 86

214

Brown Angels *20*
Brown Honey in Broomwheat Tea *14*
Caribbean Canvas *76*
Coconut Kind of Day *75*
The Cremation of Sam McGee *65*
Father and Son *18*
Hairs—Pelitos *34*
If You're Not from the Prairie... *65*
My Song Is Beautiful: Poems and Pictures in Many Voices *161*
Not a Copper Penny in Me House *74*
Paper Boats *150*
Pass It On: African-American Poetry for Children *17*
The Shooting of Dan McGrew *69*
This Same Sky: A Collection of Poems from around the World *165*
Soul Looks Back in Wonder *14*
The Tamarindo Puppy and Other Poems *85*

Political and Racial Oppression
Ajeemah and his Son *71*
Aunt Harriet's Underground Railroad in the Sky *23*
Baachan! Geechan! Arigato *42*
The Big Lie *126*
The Bracelet *43*
Chain of Fire *62*
The Clay Marble *152*
A Hand Full of Stars *142*
Haveli *150*
Journey to Jo'burg: A South African Story *62*
Kiss the Dust *140*
Many Thousand Gone *14*
Naomi's Road *41*
Nightjohn *21*
Rice without Rain *153*
Song of the Buffalo Boy *152*
Sworn Enemies *127*
Taste of Salt *79*
This Land Is My Land *108*
Year of Impossible Goodbyes *130*
Zlata's Diary: A Child's Life in Sarajevo *94*

The Refugee Experience
  Andi's War *173*
  A Boat to Nowhere *54*
  The Clay Marble *152*
  Fighters, Refugees, Immigrants: A Story of the Hmong *52*
  Goodbye Vietnam *54*
  Into a Strange Land: Unaccompanied Refugee Youth
    in America *50*
  Journey of the Sparrows *33*
  Kiss the Dust *140*
  The Lotus Seed *51*
  The Little Weaver of Thai-Yen Village *53*
  So Far from the Bamboo Grove *119*
  The Wheel of Surya *146*
  Year of Impossible Goodbyes *130*

School and Learning
  Absolutely Invincible *50*
  Aekyung's Dream *47*
  Ahyoka and the Talking Leaves *110*
  Among the Volcanoes *82*
  Angel Child, Dragon Child *53*
  The Barber's Cutting Edge *13*
  Baseball in April and Other Stories *39*
  Chi-Hoon: A Korean Girl *133*
  The Day of Ahmed's Secret *138*
  Finding My Voice *46*
  For the Life of Laetitia *74*
  If It Hadn't Been for Yoon Jun *46*
  I Hate English! *26*
  I'm New Here *37*
  Josepha: A Prairie Boy's Story *67*
  Last Summer with Maizon *24*
  The Most Beautiful Place in the World *81*
  Neve Shalom/ Wahat al-Salam: Oasis of Peace *136*
  Nightjohn *21*
  Over Here It's Different: Carolina's Story *34*
  Rio Grande Stories *164*
  The Sandwich *31*
  Song Lee in Room 2B *46*
  Spud Sweetgrass *66*
  Yang the Youngest and His Terrible Ear *28*

Shelter
   Against the Stoorm *139*
   Amish Home *31*
   The Clay Marble *152*
   House and Homes *164*
   The Village of Round and Square Houses *59*
   This Is My House *159*

Sports
   Baseball Saved Us *42*
   The Hockey Sweater *65*
   Hopscotch around the World *163*
   In the Year of the Boar and Jackie Robinson *27*
   The Magic Hockey Skates *67*
   Supergrandpa *174*
   Yang the Youngest and His Terrible Ear *28*

Stories of Courage
   The Big Lie *126*
   The Clay Marble *152*
   The Girl with the White Flag *114*
   Goodbye Vietnam *54*
   Haveli *150*
   The Hidden Children *124*
   Journey to Jo'burg: A South African Story *62*
   Kiss the Dust *140*
   Nightjohn *21*
   Number the Stars *126*
   Sadako *113*
   Sadako and the Thousand Paper Cranes *113*
   Sami and the Time of the Troubles *138*
   So Far from the Bamboo Grove *119*
   The Wheel of Surya *146*
   Year of Impossible Goodbyes *130*
   Zlata's Diary: A Child's Life in Sarajevo *94*

Strong and Resourceful Female Characters
   Amazing Grace *16*
   Among the Volcanoes *83*
   Dinner at Aunt Connie's House *22*
   Flyaway Girl *59*
   The Gift of Changing Woman *110*
   Harriet's Daughter *78*

Haveli *150*
Maizon at Blue Hill *25*
The Princess and the Beggar: A Korean Folktale *133*
Roses Sing on New Snow *29*
The Samurai's Daughter *117*
Savitri: A Tale of Ancient India *149*
Shabanu: Daughter of the Wind *149*
Sitti's Secrets *141*
The Rajah's Rice *145*
A Young Painter: The Life and Paintings of Wang Yani *91*
Zlata's Diary: A Child's Life in Sarajevo *94*

The World of Work
Abuela's Weave *82*
At the Crossroads *59*
The Barber's Cutting Edge *13*
Chicken Man *137*
The Day of Ahmed's Secret *138*
How a Shirt Grew in the Field *101*
A Kibbutz in Israel *143*
Peppe the Lamplighter *30*
The Piñata Maker/El Piñatero *81*
Radio Man: A Story in English and Spanish *35*
Roses Sing on New Snow *29*
Uncle Jed's Barbershop *20*
Voices from the Fields: Children of Migrant Farmworkers Tell Their Stories *33*